Comes A Soldier's Whisper

A Collection of Wartime Letters with Reflection and Hope for the Future

*To Nancy,
All the best,
Jenny LaSala*

Jenny La Sala

Order this book online at www.trafford.com
or email orders@trafford.com

Most Trafford titles are also available at major online book retailers.

Visit the following website to share a story or contact the author:
http://www.comesasoldierswhisper.com/

Printed in the United States of America.

ISBN: 978-1-4669-7686-3 (sc)
ISBN: 978-1-4669-7685-6 (hc)
ISBN: 978-1-4669-7687-0 (e)

Library of Congress Control Number: 2013900965

Trafford rev. 08/29/2013

 www.trafford.com

North America & international
toll-free: 1 888 232 4444 (USA & Canada)
fax: 812 355 4082

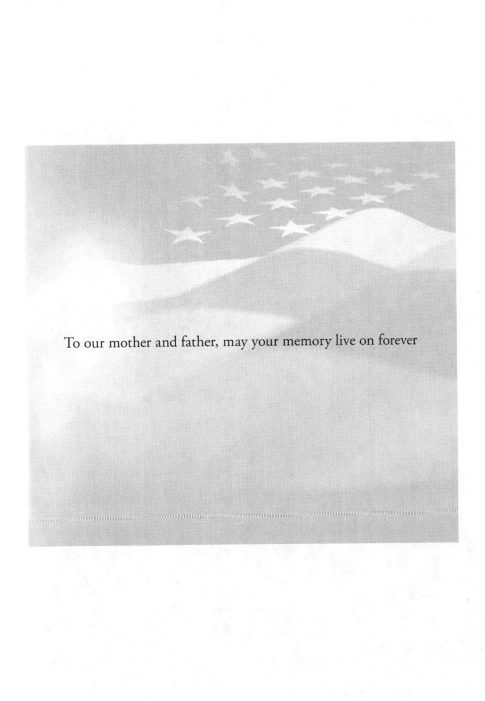

To our mother and father, may your memory live on forever

ACKNOWLEDGMENTS

I AM DEEPLY GRATEFUL and wish to express my appreciation to the following individuals who gave me technical guidance and support.

Peter Hendrikx was born in Eindhoven, Holland and has interviewed hundreds of veterans including my father. Peter is the author of Orange is the Color of the Day, a large pictorial history of the 101st Airborne liberation of his country. Peter pays tribute to soldiers buried at the U.S. Military Cemetery in Margraten, the Netherlands on his website: http://www.heroesatmargraten.com/

Richard Ladd, 101st Airborne Screaming Eagle, Five-O-Deuce PIR. Richard remembered our father, calling him and other radiomen, "The Communicators."

John (Jack) Sherman, 101st Airborne, 327 Glider Infantry. His compelling interview is featured on Kevin Brook's GLIDER INFANTRYMAN website. http://www.gliderman.com/

John Sherman is a big part of Don Rich's story in Kevin Brook's book, Glider Infantryman which is based on Don Rich, a 327

Glider Infantry Screaming Eagle. My father was in awe of these glider pilots. Mr. Don Rich passed away on May 1, 2013.

Guy Whidden, 101st Airborne Screaming Eagle and author of "Between The Lines and Beyond." His interview and book are featured on his website: http://www.guywhidden.com/

Mark Bando, author of several books on the 101st Airborne was instrumental in connecting me with WWII Veterans, some who remembered my father. Please visit Mark Bando's official website at 101airborneww2.com or join his Trigger Time Forum at http://triggertimeforum.yuku.com

———◦《(◦)》◦———

COMES A SOLDIER'S WHISPER is grateful to Operation First Response for their interest in our project.

A portion of the book's profits will be contributed to OFR to assist in their invaluable work and aide to America's veterans.

Operation First Response serves our nation's Wounded Warriors and their families with personal and financial needs. Services are provided from the onset of injury, throughout their recovery period and along their journey from military life into the civilian world.

For more information, please visit OFR at http://www.operationfirstresponse.org/

THIS BOOK WAS written in loving memory and dedication to my father, David Clinton Tharp, who served in the 101st Airborne Division (the Screaming Eagles) during WWII, and to my brother, David L. Tharp, who served in the navy and army, 101st Airborne.

WWII was a global war that was under way by 1939 and ended in 1945. This book chronicles letters written by one soldier, depicting his personal journey before, during, and after the war as a radio operator while serving under the 101st Airborne Division.

He would write, "My silk is my silent weapon and the thread upon which my life hangs." And so the sentiments of a soldier's whisper some seventy years later, a thought-provoking process to be shared by all soldiers—past, present, and future.

The Indian name *Currahee* stood for "We stand alone" and was adopted as the battle cry for the 101st Airborne Division, the Screaming Eagles. May all soldiers *stand alone together*, in times of war and peace, and travel safely and journey back home again

Dad also reflected with great sadness regarding all the men returning from war as "changed" from who they once were—some missing sight, hearing, and more often than not, limbs. And let us not forget those soldiers who returned with the invisible scars of war, as was the case of our father who moaned in his sleep for many years. But those changes cannot take away from who these men were and continue to be.

Who he is now does not take away from who he was.
It doesn't change the past.

—Amy Grant, Christian singer- songwriter
paying tribute to her father

CONTENTS

PREFACE

I WISH TO give many heartfelt thanks to Tom Brokaw whose books *The Greatest Generation* and the sequel *The Greatest Generation Speaks* gave me the inspiration to tell my father's personal story through his wartime letters written during WWII as a 101st Airborne paratrooper and radio operator.

Among many selected others, I was very fortunate to have had my thank-you letter to Mr. Brokaw and three of my father's letters published in *The Greatest Generation Speaks* in 1999, not long after my father's passing.

Mr. Brokaw's office told me how particularly impressed they were of one of my father's letters written August 9, 1945, addressing the racial problems of then and today, one of the many letters that reflect the *whisperings* of a young man who was clearly way ahead of his time.

My father was proud to be a Screaming Eagle paratrooper of the Five-O-Deuce and to fight for his country. As with most soldiers of war, they do not speak of the battle, the experience of it or the honors bestowed upon them. These letters written solely by one soldier give an insight as to what his sweetheart and family were going through back home. His written words are insightful and resonate with the soldiers of today.

Although you will not find our mother's actual letters within this collection of wartime letters, her thoughts are interwoven between the lines, as is the history of that special generation. I am proud and honored to share this collection of letters with you.

May this publication be an eternal salute of gratitude for all veterans and soldiers of war.

INTRODUCTION

A SOLDIER THINKS of important things to keep him going in battle:

- His fellow soldiers
- His family
- The *letters*

My father, David Clinton Tharp enlisted in the U.S.Army in 1943 at the age of 18. He was from Petersburg, Indiana. The Army gave additional pay as an incentive to join the paratroopers. Dad quickly signed up for the extra pay to assist his father and help support his brothers and sisters. He was then assigned to the 101st Airborne Division, one of the most elite units in the Army and was later attached to the Five-O-Deuce. He went through arduous and rigorous training before being shipped to England.

On D-Day, he was in the first wave to parachute into Normandy, France. His unit would later be sent to Carentan (Purple Heart Lane), Holland (Operation Market-Garden) and the Battle of the Bulge, for which he received the EAME Theater Ribbon with (4) Bronze Battle Stars and (1) Arrowhead, Purple Heart with Oak Leaf cluster, Presidential Unit Citations (2) for Normandy and Bastogne.

The Dutch government awarded the 101st Airborne with the Netherlands Orange Lanyard for the Holland Airborne Invasion. He was with regimental headquarters and was a radio communicator for Colonel Cole, Colonel Michaelis and Colonel Chappuis. He would later receive the Bronze Star Medal for meritorious service in action from June 6th to December 28, 1944.

Due to strict Army censorship rules, he could say nothing about his many operations or locations . . . But when the war ended, the veil of censorship was lifted, and he was able to vent and tell how he was wounded for the first time and could express resentment and how bad the war had been. His hope for a return home is poignant, as he writes about life, marriage, children and a home. This book was written to preserve my father's wartime letters and to serve as a family memoir. But in the process, the book seemed to take on a life of its' own with sentiments that resonate with all soldiers of the past, present and future. Our family is very proud to present and share Comes A Soldier's Whisper and a peek into the life of one soldier's heart and thoughts during the greatest generation.

Please be aware that some aspects of these letters reflect fear, anger, and sometimes even hatred for the enemy both during and immediately following the war and is not meant to slight anyone or any group of people or nations. Such could be compared to a soldier's feelings toward the enemy of any given war—past, present, or future—such as the wars in Vietnam, Korea, Iraq, and Afghanistan, just to name a few.

The *letters* are one of the best things we can do until our soldiers return home again. As time goes by, hopefully, a soldier's letters will be preserved and find a home, as our father's letters have found a final resting place in this book. I discovered that my father's best letters, written to his then sweetheart, Betty Lou, who later became his wife and our mother, to be filled with personal reflections of the war and written after the war ended and during his time in Austria with the occupation of the Germans, June to December 1945. All the intricate personal letters, as written by many lovers, were set aside and not included in this book out of respect and honor to our parents' privacy. The constant flow of letters sent during the war kept his sanity and spirits alive for this soldier who developed a war heart through his battle experiences. His photos both before and after battle reveal the changes that he writes about in some of his letters, saying, "I'm amazed at my life and body intact."

The *whisperings* of those feelings felt and perhaps not heard as loudly after the war, as opposed to those heard during the war itself, are very revealing and deserve a voice and recognition. I believe that this is an important venue. Every soldier shares similar thoughts about family and the future, privately wondering what awaits them upon returning home.

My childhood memories left a lasting impression of looking at Dad's wartime medals kept in a drawer—the musty smell of the leather cases they were in, lined with red satin, opening them with wonder and pride, even at our young age. Dad never got upset at our pulling out his medals from time to time. I now wonder what was going through his mind as we sifted through his accomplishments. We somehow knew not to ask too many questions. His sadness of losing his younger sister, mother, and father when he was only ten, twelve, and nineteen, respectively, leaving him as the eldest of four younger siblings, extended beyond explanation or what words could express.

Dad also kept photographs of the Holocaust and genocide concentration camps from WWII, Dachau in particular. When we asked why, he replied, "Because one day, people will say it never happened, and I have proof that it did." Those photographs captured in the book entitled *Dachau* and published by the American army after the war in 1945 was later donated in 1999 to the Holocaust Memorial Resource Museum (www.holocaustedu. org) in Maitland, Florida. In addition, our mother, who was a wonderful sculptress, also donated her work entitled *I Accuse*, representing a Holocaust concentration camp survivor, and is also on display at the same museum.

May this book be a place where soldiers of yesterday, today, and tomorrow can reflect many of the same timeless sentiments from one soldier to another.

My father will always be my hero. The older I get, I realize that he was the biggest influence in my life. It is with tremendous pride that I offer this collection of wartime letters to be shared with other children and their heroes of that great generation and those to follow.

In memory of all the men and women who serve to protect the United States with the following oath of enlistment, both in peacetime and wartime, to protect and maintain the liberty and freedom that our forefathers fought for, may we take this and every opportunity to say a special thank-you to all our veterans:

> I do solemnly swear that I will support and defend the Constitution of the United States against all enemies, foreign and domestic; that I will bear true faith and allegiance to the same; and that I will obey the orders of the President of the United States and the orders of the officers appointed over me, according to regulations and the Uniform Code of Military Justice. So help me God.

Let us all take a moment and stand in silence for those who protect us and keep us from harm's way in the past, present, and future of this country.

CHAPTER 1

JUST A COUNTRY BOY

He's just a country boy
With a smile as bright as the rising sun

He's just a country boy
As tall and straight as he can be
With the strength and majesty of the great oak tree
That stands ever watchful by the farm

He's just a country boy
His demands are very few
A wife, a farm, and children too
He must have at least one

A simple, honest country boy
To sow and reap and reap and sow
And be just a country boy

—Betty Lou

US ARMY AIR FORCES
Technical Training School
Lowry Field, Colorado

January 15, 1943

Dear Betty Lou,

Today I just received your letter from which you mailed the 8th of December, even though it's just been a month getting to me. I'm proud to get it, for it was a wonderful letter. You're still making mistakes on that typewriter though. Ha-ha. I'm just kidding you. Just keep right on the job, and someday, you'll be a swell typist.

I'm sorry I let you worry of my whereabouts, as you mentioned in your letter. But golly, we were busy out there in California. It would have been all right if you had wrote my father about me, for he knows where I was. I would have been all right anyway, for Dad knows I write to you all of the time. I'll bet he would even know you if he met you on the street, for there is an enlarged picture of you at home on the radio.

I'm sorry I didn't get this letter before Christmas, for you asked me what I wanted for Christmas. Well, I wouldn't have known, and you did a wonderful job of selecting a gift anyway. Say, it was swell of you to buy that with your own money. I hope you still have your part-time job.

Betty Lou, you asked me what "shipped off" meant. It means that we're on shipping orders and ready to be shipped out at any time of the day or night.

You said your mother sent me a Christmas card. Tell her I said many, many thanks for thinking of me. I haven't received it as yet, but I probably will, for I've been getting quite a bit of mail from

Fresno lately. So I'm hoping to get it soon. I haven't received yours either. But even if I don't, I'll know that you sent me one.

I didn't know anyone read the letters I sent you. And as you say, your mother likes me just by the way I write. I thought I was very poor at writing letters. She must be a very nice person. I'm sure she is, and someday in the future, I'd like to have the opportunity to meet her. I'll bet you're just the very picture of her, aren't you?

I'm sorry you lost the picture of me in my CCC[1] uniform. The only one I have left is an enlarged one. But in a few days, I'll send you a better one, for I had my pictures taken today. I can't get the kind of work done that I wanted though. But later on, I'll have some more taken and send you a nice picture. I must close for today. So until I hear from you, which is very soon I hope. I remain.

As ever,
David

PS: The sweetheart on the envelope[2] hardly fits, I guess. But I have to send it to someone. And I think a lot of you, so I suppose it'll be all right.

---

[1]   During the Great Depression, CCC stood for Civilian Conservation Corps. This government program was the part of President Franklin Roosevelt's New Deal effort that dealt with alleviating severe unemployment in the United States. The program ran from 1933 to 1942. Dad entered the service through Fort Benjamin in Harrison, Indiana. After completing basic training, he transferred to technical training in Colorado.

[2]   See envelope photo in "Campaign, Battles, and Photographs" section.

Petersburg, Indiana
March 11, 1943

1:20 a.m.

Dearest,

Just a few words tonight as I'm very sleepy. I've been up for almost four whole nights, and I'm very tired.

You are probably wondering why I'm at home in the States. Please believe, darling, it's hard to say. But I happened to be at home on an emergency furlough of ten days. You see, my father has passed away. I'm very sorry I haven't answered your letter as yet. But Dad has been very ill for the last week. And I've been writing to him every day.

I received your letter last Saturday and Sunday night; I received a telegram about Dad. So Monday, I was on my way home. Tuesday morning, I was in Chicago. God, but I'd like to see you. But I don't suppose I will this time.

For as you know, now that both my mother and father are gone, a lot is left up to me. I think I can fix things so that my brothers and sisters can stay together. And I want to stay here until everything is straightened out.

Well, dear, I must close now and get some sleep in a few minutes as Dad is to be laid away tomorrow.

As ever,
David

Location Unknown
March 22, 1943

My Dearest Betty,

A few lines tonight to let you know I'm thinking of you. As usual, I always am for that matter. I hope this letter finds everyone well and happy and going to school, ha-ha. But just think, darling, you haven't got so very much more to go. Then you will be through.

Well, things are going pretty good here now. There was a new bunch of students came in while I was gone. But they seem to be a pretty good bunch and are willing to learn and do as they are told. That's what it takes. Well, so much for the students.

Darling, I don't believe I told you about my buddies. There are four of us: Johnny, Dick, and Ted, with me being the fourth one. We are really quite a bunch.

I have your picture out tonight, and Johnny asked if he might write you a short note, and I said he might if I approve of it. Ha-ha. Honest kid, he is a darn swell pal. We are all privates but Ted, and he is a corporal. But he is the same as us when we are together.

Betty, I will close for tonight as I want to send you a poem that I think is very good. I don't think I ever sent you a copy of it.

Forever yours with love,
David

United States Air Forces
Lowry Field, Colorado
April 19, 1943

My Dearest Darling,

Received your letter today and was very happy to hear from you.

I'm being honest with you when I say I have a different outlook on life since I've met you. Somehow, you've changed things for me. Everything seems brighter now, and may God permit our hearts to beat as one someday.

Dearest, as for a tough road to travel in the paratroopers, I'm not worried. I'm just waiting and waiting and getting in better shape every day. Believe me, I am. I weigh 178 lbs. now and not exactly a softie. As for jujitsu, it isn't exactly new to me. And my boxing would come in handy perhaps. So don't worry your beautiful head over me. I'll be all right. You just keep the home fire burning.

Betty Lou, it makes me feel grand to know that things I send and say please you. I'm grateful with all my heart that I have you. Thank you, my dear, when you say that I get handsomer every day. I have an album with a few pictures in it and will send it to you, for things like that are too much trouble to keep around your personal belongings. Anyway, I'd rather you keep it.

I received a letter from a schoolmate today. Our track team won their two meets so far. I'd give anything to be back there this spring to run the mile. I could do it too, as good a shape as I'm in. They haven't got a man this year that's very good, not that I am. But I could help out.

Dearest, I wouldn't say you are the luckiest girl in the world, just to know a fellow like me. I'm no angel. I'm just a plain raised farm boy from Southern Indiana who loves a girl named Betty Lou.

Although I could write on and on, I must close now. I have to study my lesson for school. We are learning about dehydrated foods. It's very interesting even though I don't care so much about it.

With all my love,
David

Lowry Field
Denver, Colorado

May 18, 1943

My Dearest Darling,

Received the book yesterday, a million thanks. I've wanted to read it for quite awhile but just neglected getting it. I've read part of it already, and it's swell.

Well, dear, there isn't much to say today except that I still love you 100 percent, that is important to me. Our little mascot is a 160-pound St. Bernard dog and bit "5" of the fellows yesterday. He's no damn pet of mine. I stay away from him.

Did I ever tell you about our new dayroom? If not, I will. It's pretty nice with a pool table, tennis table, reading racks, writing desks, radio, and mail room—almost anything a person could ask for.

Well, sweetheart, I'll close for today. As it is 4:15 and I have to get ready and march some students to work.

Love as ever,
David

Lowry Field
Denver, Colorado

June 3, 1943

My Dearest,

Golly, I'm a few days behind in answering your letter, which I received Monday.

Darling, I'm sorry, but you see, I'm going to school again in instructor's class this time. My sergeant and I are both going this week. And we have two majors for class instructors. And how one of them is from Washington, DC, and the other is from Ft. Riley, Kansas, B & C School. They're tough, and to my opinion, a few of the boys will cease to be instructors. However, I'm doing okay. It ends tomorrow, and am I ever glad.

Darling, I'm proud of you for selling those bonds.[3] If only everyone would do that, for it's equipment we need now and not men. Of course, we are getting more and more every day. It won't be long now. At least, I hope not. That's a swell drive your school is putting on.

Well, I better close for now as it is time to go to work. Boy, we've really had some changes around here. Please write soon as I'll be waiting for a letter from you.

Love always,
David

---

[3] War bonds are government-issued savings bonds, which are used to finance a war or a military action. In the United States, the last official war bond was the Series E bond issued during the Second World War. War bonds generate capital for the federal government, and they make civilians feel involved in their national militaries. Exhortations to buy war bonds are often accompanied with appeals to patriotism and conscience.

US Army Air Forces
Technical Training School
Lowry Field, Colorado

June 5, 1943

My Dearest Only,

Golly, it was good to hear from you as I haven't heard for a few days. It's always good to hear from you though.

I'm happy to know that the bond drive was a success. At least some people are doing their share at home. You said in your letter, darling, that I probably wouldn't be here to receive your letter. Well, I was. But I'll be subject to leave any day now. Everything is completed at last, and we are waiting for orders.

Darling, you're not the only one who hopes I get through my training all right. So do I. Yes, I know just what you mean about being washed out. I've lost several students from my shift already. But if you can't carry the load, you're just not any good in that branch of service.

However, it's only natural for one to wonder and worry. I do. I guess it's the waiting that is getting me down. However, I'm not afraid. I can make it. I know only too well that it will be tougher and much worse than you realize. Of course, I'm in good condition. I do a little jumping, running, and exercise every day.

I hope you did all right in your play. But, darling, I can't see you playing the part of a widow. But perhaps you will fit all right. But I could find a part much better for you.

Well, sweetheart, I'd better close as I have a million things to do, none as important as this letter, I can assure you. So good-bye for now and may we see each other soon.

Love always,
David

US Army Air Forces
Technical Training School
Lowry Field, Colorado

August 26, 1943

My Dearest Darling,

Hope you'll not be angry at me for not writing any this week.

But now that I'm really on the beam, I'll write a few lines. By the way, they're playing *No Letter Today* over the loudspeaker from the office, and it's the Hoosier Hot Shots playing. Boy, I'm right at home.

I'm very happy just knowing that you're back home waiting on me and dreaming of the future and working. That means more to me, probably more than you'll ever know, for I often think of the future with you and a little one with it.

Say, guess what happened today? My first sergeant said, "Are you still ready to leave us next month, boy?" I jumped and said, "Yes, sir," ha-ha. Anyway, it sure made me happier. He said they had another letter on me. So now, you can see why I'm on the beam again and feeling fine.

Betty, I suppose I'd better close now as I have to attend an aircraft picture tonight, so I'll have to hurry. So, darling, please write me, once a week at least, if possible, for I love to hear from you.

Love always,
David

United States Paratrooper Stationery

September 20, 1943

My Darling Betty,

Well, today was the happiest day I've had for a week as I finally received a letter from you.

Yes, darling, I knew all the time just when I was leaving to come down here. But for some reason, I didn't want to tell you and, about halfway, told you that I wasn't coming at all. But now that I am here, please forgive me. I am very glad that you realize that being a paratrooper is what I want and many thanks for wishing me luck. I'll need every bit you wish me.

Well, I have gone into "B" stage training today with my class. My injury didn't keep me back. Thank God for that. Honey, you seem to think that there is lots of tough work down here. Well, there is. It is rough. But don't make it too bad. I'm getting along okay and am pretty sure I'll make it. Darling, my chin is up very high, and as far as my training goes, I'll keep it there until they knock it down.

You asked when I would start jumping. My first jump from a real plane will be October 4, 1943. Today, I started jumping from a 34-foot tower in a parachute harness. Next week, I'll go to the 250-foot towers[4] with a real chute and plenty of excitement. On

---

[4]   Army paratrooper training location airborne school is held at Fort Benning in Columbus, Georgia. Airborne trainees are housed in the airborne barracks during training. The location of the training is on the main post at Fort Benning and can be easily identified by the 250-foot-tall airborne towers. Airborne training is three weeks long, though some soldiers may be on holdover for several weeks, waiting for a training slot in the school. Somewhere along the line,

the 34-foot tower, you climb up a ladder and to a platform and then step to a door, which represents a plane door. Then the sergeant hollers "go," and you jump out. You fall about 15 feet and get a hell of a jerk, which represents the opening shock of a real parachute. After that, you get a nice, gentle ride on down to the ground and land. It's quite a lot of fun.

Although some of the boys didn't think so and wouldn't jump out into space. But I guess I'm crazy enough to try anything once. Then they strapped me in a parachute harness and let me ride down an incline of about 60 degrees until I reached a speed of about 10 miles per hour. Then they dropped me, and I dropped about 4 feet, landing on my feet and tumbling. That's all there is to it. It's a little work now and then but lots of fun.

Darling, you asked me to tell you what my grandmother thought of my being down here. Well, I don't think she has the right idea of what I do with the parachute. By that, I don't think she knows that I'll jump from a plane with one on. And I'll not tell her either.

Well, sweet, I'd better close as I have to shine my boots, which is a nightly task. Sending you all my love and best wishes to you.

Always yours,
David

Dad was changed over from the Air Force to Army Paratroopers most likely as replacement to fallen soldiers overseas.

US Parachute Troops
October 10, 1943

My Dearest Darling,

A few words before I move. I'm shipping this afternoon at 2:30.
So you need not write until you hear from me. I'm not moving
from this post. I'm going to school. Two other boys and myself
are Hoosiers. How about that, honey?

We will be at school from three to nine weeks. I'll have to make
two or three more jumps while I'm here. So much the better for
me though. The more experience, the better for me.

Darling, I'm sending you a miniature set of wings. Wear them as
I would mine, for they're the best ones in the world. At least, we
think so around here.

Darling, I must close as I have to be outside in a few minutes.
Write soon.

Love always,
David

Paratroops
Fort Benning, Georgia

October 19, 1943

My Darling Betty Lou,

I received your letter today and sure was glad as I was expecting it. But then, I'm always looking for one from you.

Haven't got much time as I have to go back to class for two hours tonight. I go to school eight hours a day and two hours on Tuesday and Thursday nights. So, darling, I don't think you would get to see me if you got to come down. I'm sure you haven't gotten my letter yet asking you to come and visit me on Christmas.

Please, darling, say you will come, wherever I'm at. I'll probably be around Fort Benning someplace, I hope. But after January and February, I wouldn't say where I would be, if you know what I mean. But so much for that now.

Darling, I'm glad you received the wings, emblem, and pillowcase. The one I picked out had Sweetheart on it. Yes, darling, there were two paratroopers killed here last week. I hoped and hoped that you would not see it in the papers. I knew you probably would though. Please try not to think about it.

It would make this soldier very happy if you said yes to one little question. I'm quite sure things would go okay, darling. I just hope the wedding dress won't be made out of a parachute though, if you ever do give your consent to the question.

Darling, I must close now as I have to go. Please write soon.

Yours always,
David

United States Army
Signal Corps
Pigeon Section

November 10, 1943

My Darling,

Just a few lines this afternoon. I received your letter today. I don't remember just how long it has been since I've had one.

You probably think it odd of me using this stationery. I'm now at the signal corps here at the main post, learning about pigeons[5] as they plan an important part in communications. I had a few spare minutes, so I got the paper off of one of the boys.

Well, honey, I must close. I make a jump tomorrow, I suppose. The sergeant hasn't said so as yet. But I'm sure I'll be the man to do it.

Write soon, my dear, and don't worry.

Always yours,
David

---

[5] During the D-day invasion of World War II, many soldiers were sent with a pigeon beneath their coats. This was a period of radio silence, so the use of pigeons for relaying messages was optimal. The pigeons were able to send back information on German gun positions on the Normandy beaches. Thirty-two pigeons were awarded the prestigious Dickin Medal, Britain's highest award for animal valor. Recipients included a bird named G. I. Joe, who flew twenty miles in twenty minutes with a message that stopped US planes from bombing an Italian town that was occupied by British forces. Army Pigeons in World War I and II | Suite101.

CHAPTER II

Sea Transport—Location Unknown

I am a soldier, I fight where I am told,
and I win where I fight.

—General George S. Patton Jr.,
American Commander, WWII

502ⁿᵈ Paratroop Infantry
Location Unknown
January 3, 1944

My Darling,

I didn't really mean to scare you about what I said last night when I called. I was sorry after it. But it was too late then. Guess you may as well know, I have great possibilities of going overseas. In fact, I am on a shipment. When or where I'll go, I know no more than you. Wherever I go darling, you're right with me.

I hated to send the enlargement back to you. But there was nothing else I could do. I would have had to part with it later, and this way is best. The other pictures and personal things I'm not allowed to have. The wings, darling, wear them always and think of me. I'll come back to you someday. My only regret is that I can't leave you as my wife. But of course, there are many things to consider, I know.

I called your mother a little while ago. It was good to hear her voice. I had a million things to say. But I couldn't say anything. I even forgot my real purpose of why I called her. There is only one public telephone in the area. And there is no telegraph for V-mail.

You're allowed only so much time, and you must have someone with you. In other words, we are restricted to the area. Where I'm at doesn't really matter. My address is a little different now. So notice it.

Darling, I guess I better close for now. Please write and often. Hon, write soon and write me often. I will write as often as possible.

Always yours,
David

Location Unknown
January 4, 1944

My Darling,

I'll try and write a few lines this morning. They were kind enough to not make us do anything this morning after keeping us up late last night.

No mail from you yesterday, in fact, none for several days now. Perhaps it's because I have moved. I hope so. I may as well get used to it, for there will be times later when I probably won't receive any mail for weeks the way we move around. We never stay in one place.

Hope this finds everyone well. I am fine. Darling, please don't worry about me. I can take care of myself and have for several years now.

Darling, I must close for now. I'll try and write later.

Always yours.

Love,
David

Location Unknown
January 5, 1944

My Darling,

Here are more of my pictures.

I'm not allowed to take them with me. The reason is that they show I'm a paratrooper.

Take care of everything and yourself, darling.

Love,
David

Location Unknown
January 21, 1944

My Darling,

Gee, today I received two letters from Fort Benning, Georgia, all from you. I guess they are catching up with me, and am I ever glad. It's so good to hear from you.

Hon, the time I called you from Fort Benning and said I wasn't going across. I said that because I didn't want you to worry. But I guess I didn't explain enough when I said I was sending your pictures back. I'm sorry.

Darling, don't ever think there is someone else; there never has been and never will be anyone that can take your place in my life that means to me what you do. I was so mixed up when I called you, for I knew my number had come up. I knew it meant leaving you behind.

After reading this letter from you, darling, well, the way you explained fate and destiny, it just made me feel better. Of course I'm coming back. I've got to. But I'd rather not talk about it.

About the little boy, darling, he is in my billfold. He'll stay there until I come back. And, hon, he does remind me of you and our future so much, a picture of health and happiness. Darling, what you said in your letter about me being wounded (if I should, it made a lump come into my throat), if only every girl felt that way. Then many of the boys would come home happier. Everyone gives that subject a lot of thought. I promise not to worry about it.

Sweetheart, I must close for now. I just don't have time. Will write as often as possible.

Love always,
David

Location Unknown
January 27, 1944

My Darling,

Just a few lines tonight as I probably won't be writing for a few days, but so much for that.

Darling, I'm sending a couple of pictures. I know you'll get a laugh out of them. The one of the three of us was taken at a phony place. I mean, the bottles are empty and a false background. But they look quite real, especially the one with the cigarette in my mouth. But keep them, my dear, and we'll get a laugh out of them together someday.

I got you a Valentine tonight. I know it's early, but I probably won't have another chance to get you one after this. I hope you like it.

Well, this isn't much of a letter. But a few words are better than none at all. There is no need for you to write here after you receive this letter. I'll write as soon as possible.

Yours always,
David

Location Unknown
US Army Stationery
February 4, 1944

My Darling,

Gee, but you've been swell in your letters, only I haven't received any from you for well over a week now.

But I haven't written either, not because I haven't heard from you, but because we were told not to write to anyone. Anyway, I am writing a little when I can and save it and send it when I can. God knows when it will be, not until I'm overseas. But at least you will know that I'm thinking of you. It's beautiful out tonight. The stars are out, and there is almost a full moon, sort of cool, like early spring.

You know, darling, it's disgusting not being able to talk about anything. I don't like the news in the papers. It seems that in Washington, DC, they want to take our extra $50 away from us for a while. It wouldn't surprise me if they take it away from us altogether. They can do that. But they can't take our pride away from us.

The spirit and morale in this outfit is greater than any I know of. We're all damn proud to be what we are. People talk about us, call us glamour boys, USO[6] kids, and God knows what not. But how many of those people who talk about us would go through what we do for what we get? Not one in a hundred.

Well, sweetheart, I must close for tonight and will write more later. Good night, darling, and God bless you.

Always yours.
Love,
David

---

[6] A group of women and men dedicated to preserving the history of the United Service Organizations (USO) during the World War Two time period. WW2 USO—Stateside Operations—Living History.

Location Unknown
US Army Stationery
February 10, 1944

Hello Darling,

Well, after a week, I'm back again on paper. I'm sorry I haven't wrote any, but it's been almost impossible to write because of conditions, too damn rocky for anything except to rock you to sleep.

We've dropped anchor at some port. But I won't say where. Someday, I can tell you about the trip. I've liked it swell so far and haven't gotten seasick either. But, oh, some of these guys got really sick. Guess I should have been a sailor as well as I like the water. But then you never would've agreed to that, would you?

I wonder how the weather is at home. It's cold and snowing here where I am. I just came down off the deck. But that's the kind of weather I like though I would like to be on land when it's like that. The snow sort of reminds me of Colorado.

We were given Red Cross packages the other day, and what a surprise. Many of them were from Gary, Indiana. Mine was also. It at least shows that the Red Cross stuff does get around.

Well, my darling, I will close for now and will write the next chance I get. Remember, I love you with all my heart. Keep the home fires burning. I'll be back soon.

Always yours.

Love,
David

Location Unknown
V-Mail
February 24, 1944

My Dearest,

Gee, today was quite a day, and the reason for that is because I received some mail—three from you, two from your mother, and two from home.

It's sure good to hear from everyone. And some of the letters the boys get, honest, we really get a laugh with the newspaper clippings about paratroopers and all.

Darling, no matter what comes up, don't worry and keep your chin up like a trooper's sweetheart should. Guess I've got things on the ball now, saving all of my money, putting it into war bonds and the bank also.

Well, dearest, I must close. You can't write much on this paper. I'll write a regular letter once in awhile.

Always yours.

Love,
David

Location Unknown
V-Mail
February 27, 1944

My Darling,

A few lines today to the sweetest girl in the world, at least I think so.

Today is Sunday again. No one from my unit went to church this morning. But we did sing a few songs and gave our thoughts to God and our loved ones back home. It's quite amazing as to how one's thoughts turn to religion. But things over here are enough to do that.

I went to an Irish concert the other night. It was really good and the first time I enjoyed myself for quite awhile. Their concerts are quite different from ours. I'll tell you about it one of these days.

Write soon and often darling, and don't forget the pictures of us.

Yours forever.

Love,
David

Location Unknown
V-Mail
February 29, 1944

My Darling,

I received a letter from you yesterday. But gee, hon, you seem so downhearted. I hardly know what to say.

You shouldn't feel like you do about the future. Suppose I felt that way?[7] Why, things just wouldn't click. After all, darling, I'll be back in a year or so, and that really isn't long, that is, if I can come back, and I'm sure I will. Listen, my darling, I'm not reckless like I used to be. I've calmed down a lot in the last few months. And no doubt will be even quieter than before. But the less you say, the more trouble you stay out of.

Don and I went to [censored] Sunday afternoon. It's a pretty nice place. But you still can't enjoy yourself. We went to the show, had dinner, and came back. By the way, honey, Don is married.

I hope that your letter will be continued, darling, for it stopped all of a sudden.

Love,
David

---

[7] The moral of a soldier is critical to keeping his spirit intact.

Still at Sea
February [date censored], 1944

My Darling,

Just a few lines tonight. Life is normal now once again. Everyone is getting used to the sea, or most of them.

Just heard a song, which I like to hear very much. But I always have to change two words of it, so it will fit you, for you, my darling, have brown eyes. So I can't say blue eyes. There's a loudspeaker system aboard ship, and they give us the news every day, and we hear familiar songs throughout the day. Every night we hear a special service broadcast. The officers and enlisted men aboard put this on, and it's really pretty good. They have quiz programs and songs, etc.

An hour of the morning and one hour in the afternoon, we are required to go on the main deck for fresh air. But when weather permits, the fellow who sleeps below me is always up more than that. He used to be in the navy. So through him, I've acquired a small knowledge of the sea. I said small. But it's interesting and passes away the time.

Darling, I hope you write as often and regular as possible. For it is one of the best things[8] you can do for me until I come home. And it only takes a few minutes of your time.

For tonight, I will close. Good night, and God keep you, my darling.

Love forever,
David

---

[8] Here it is, in a soldier's own words: the best thing that family can do to keep his moral up is to write letters.

At Sea
February [date censored], 1944

My Darling,

Well, hon, it looks like I'll be on good old land by tomorrow, and I'll be glad of it. The sea is okay, but give me the land or air.

Life sure gets pretty dull after the first few days of travel, no excitement, and that I don't like. But there's nothing I can do about it. [Censored] I don't know as yet, and I don't know whether I will be able to tell where I'm at once I get there or not. Guess it won't make much difference.

Have you heard from my folks lately? I suppose not though. They don't write very much—period. I guess it's just as well as long as I know they are well.

This is all for now, darling.

Love forever,
David

Location Unknown
V-Mail
March 9, 1944

My Darling,

Well, hon, I'm back in the infantry again, and I feel better about it, so it's not like it was. I've run across a few fellows I know and feel right at home again (almost). I can't really feel that way until I am finally back home, but that will have to wait.

Are you receiving my letters, darling? I hope so. I write as often as I have time. It's been quite some time now since I've received any mail at all. So I should have several letters from you once it catches up with me—soon, I hope.

I'm writing this over at the Red Cross canteen, and it's really nice. The room I'm in has different colored parachutes hanging up in it, really makes it look good.

Please write often, sweetheart. Tell everyone hello for me.

Love forever,
David

England
April 1944

My Dearest,

A few lines to let you know I'm okay. I hope this finds you the same and also the rest of your family.

I went to the show last night and saw *No Time For Love*. I had seen it before, but it was good to see it again anyway. I also saw the *Dead End Kids*. Boy, they are a riot. I like them.

Darling, I received those snapshots. You'll never know how happy I was to get them. They turn back the pages of time, the most wonderful days of my life. I hope to continue them soon, and this time forever upon my return home. It will be so good to get back.

This is Sunday again, and, hon, I didn't go to church. I'm ashamed of myself. But you know I just slept too late. I received two letters from my grandmother today, and she says hello.

She can never be repaid for what she has done for me and what she is doing for my younger brothers and sisters,[9] keeping them together and everything since both my parents are now gone.

Sweetheart, I must close for now. Write often, and remember, I love you.

Yours forever,
David

---

[9] My great-grandmother Amelia, my father's grandmother, took in all his five siblings after his father died in 1943 from a heart attack. His father made him promise to keep all the kids together and avoid adoption should anything happen to him.

England
April 20, 1944

My Dearest,

Today has been a wonderful day, darling, and why? Because I received the large pictures and a letter from you. I like the pictures very much.

You seem to be looking at something far, far away, sort of dreaming like. But, oh, that smile, and the picture of us together—you look so proud.

I hope you have received the little pictures I sent you, darling. The boys say I look like a German. I hope you don't think so.

I received a letter from my younger brother, Billy Joe, today, two pages, and boy, does he sling the ink. Oh yes, he surely does not realize where I'm at, for he said, "Good luck with the Japs and wipe the saps off the map."

Those kids are growing up right under me. It seems like I've hardly spent any time with them for the last four years, and hardly, I haven't.

I hope to be back home soon, but only God knows how soon.

My darling, I must close for now. Write often as possible.

Always yours,
David

England
Easter Sunday
April 1944

My Dearest,

I hope this letter finds you well and happy on this beautiful Easter Sunday.

I hope and pray that on next Easter day, we should be together, my darling. It seems that last year has just flown by. I didn't even realize that my little sister's birthday had passed until I got a letter from home today. They're all quite well, by the way. Betty got a new dress for her birthday. I'll bet she's really proud of it. She usually is of something like that.

I received a card and letter from you today and also a letter from your mother. We had Easter services this morning, darling, and I went. I wonder if you did. Our service was swell. I'll tell you about it someday. It was very short. But I hardly think anyone regretted going. It was held on a hillside, and the grass is very green, and around the pulpit, there were brightly colored parachutes draped around. It looked really nice.

May we be together soon.

Yours forever, love and kisses,

David

CHAPTER III

MY SILK IS MY SILENT WEAPON

*We few, we happy few, we band of brothers; For he today
that sheds his blood with me; Shall be my brother.*

—William Shakespeare,
English playwright and poet

In the following pages, you will find that our Father in the midst
of and after 4 horrific battles, chose not to write about them to
avoid upsetting his family or sweetheart back home and avoid
censorship.

England
May 3, 1944

My Darling,

I went to a show last night; *Night Is Ending* was the picture. I didn't like it very well. That picture *Sahara* you spoke of, it seems ages since I saw that. As I remember, it is a good picture.

Darling, have you drawn up any plans for that little home of ours? If not, get on the ball, or I'll be way ahead of you. If you have any ideas, why don't you send me a sketch? I know that's future thinking, but I like to think of it. Although we may never have the things we plan for, it doesn't hurt to think of them. Remember, you told me how many children we are to have? However, I hardly believe I agreed, or did I?

I had a letter from home, and the kid I used to run around with was burned pretty badly and is in the Washington Hospital. I was sure sorry to hear that as he was a fine chap.

So you started a bank account? Good for you. Keep it up. I started on a few months ago, and it's really amazing how it adds up.

Ever hear about a man whose life hangs by a thread? Well, my silk (parachute) is my silent weapon, and my life hangs by its thread.

Well, darling, guess I'd better close.

Forever yours,
David

France
V-Mail
June 15, 1944

My Darling,

I hope this finds you well and happy. So far, I'm okay and doing fine.

Sorry I haven't been able to write you, but I've been just a little too busy. I'm sure you have heard about it. How is Mother and Dad and your sisters, Barbara and Virginia? Say hello for me.

I received a V-mail from you today, the first mail I've had for quite some time, and I sure was happy to get it.

Well, darling, tomorrow is my birthday. It sure has rolled around. Wish I could spend it with you. A year ago, I never dreamed I would spend it in France.

I must close for now, sweetheart. There is very little I can say. I will write when I can. Well, so long for now.

With all my love,
Dave

France
V-Mail
June 16, 1944

My Darling,

Just a few lines today. I received a V-mail from you again last night and also one from home. It sure was good to get them on my birthday.

So you're going to get another job? I do hope it's a good one, darling, and as you said, I wouldn't like for you to work in the mill unless you could work close to your father.

Well, darling, I must close for now. Don't worry about me. I'm getting along okay now. It was hell the first few days. But that's worn off a little now.

Write often, and remember, I love you.

With all my love,
David

France
V-Mail
June 17, 1944

My Dearest,

May I drop in for a little while? I have a little bit of time, so I'll say a word or two.

No letter today although the mail did come through. I received a birthday card from home, but after reading it, I had to laugh, as did my buddies, for it didn't fit my situation so very good. But it was a swell card anyway.

Guess you'll be out of school by the time you get this, darling. I sure wish I could be there. But I'm in a much different place than the gaiety and fun that will be there. I hope you have a good time, darling, and I wish you all the luck and success in the world.

For now I must close with all my love.

Forever yours,
David

France
V-Mail
June 18, 1944

My Darling,

Well, today is Sunday and a day of rest for me. Yes, we get a rest now and then. For a while, I didn't think so, but we do.

I should have gone to church services this morning. But somehow, I didn't feel just right in going after going through so many things I've seen recently. Perhaps I'll start again after everything is all over, if I can bring myself to it. But why bore you with my troubles?

Perhaps you'd like to know what this country is like. Well, darling, I'll have to start on another V-mail page and start anew.

Love and kisses,
Dave

France
V-Mail
June 18, 1944

Darling,

There isn't much I can say here about this country.

The countryside is covered with hedgerows much the same as England only the hedges are higher and the fields are smaller. They have their small villages, which seem rather nice, or rather I should say, I imagined they used to be.

The people seem very glad that we are here. But my French not being very good, I can't understand but damn little. I've been taking some pictures of everyday life, some of my buddies, and me.

Love and kisses,
David

France
V-Mail
June 20, 1944

Hello Mom,

We have been over here in France.

I suppose you've heard through the news broadcast or in the papers about what the troopers have been doing over here.[10] Well, here is a bit of news. I'll bet you haven't heard that way.

Our unit has been awarded the Presidential Citation for extraordinary service and heroism in performing our duties on June 6, 1944, something to be proud of.

Well, I must close for now. Give my love to Betty and kiss her once for me. I'll be back someday soon, and then I'll kiss her myself.

Love to all,
David

---

10   D-Day—Operation Neptune.
The 101st Airborne Division first saw combat during the Normandy invasion, 6 June 1944. The division, as part of the VII Corps assault, jumped in the dark morning before H-Hour to seize positions west of Utah Beach. Given the mission of anchoring the corps' southern flank, the division was also to eliminate the German's secondary beach defenses, allowing the seaborne forces of the 4th Infantry Division, once ashore, to continue inland. The SCREAMING EAGLES were to capture the causeway bridges that ran behind the beach between St. Martin-de-Varreville and Pouppeville. In the division's southern sector, it was to seize the la Barquette lock and destroy a highway bridge northwest of the town of Carentan and a railroad bridge farther west. At the same time, elements of the division were to establish two bridgeheads on the Douve River at le Port, northeast of Carentan. The 101st Airborne Division During WW II—Overview.

Somewhere in France
V-Mail
June 21, 1944

My Darling,

Well, hon, how are you today? Now I now that's a devil of a question to ask, for I won't get an answer for weeks. But that's life.

Darling, there isn't much I can tell you about my life here in France. I understand that I can say I did jump into combat over France to you.

I was in the rough of it for a while. That was one parachute ride I'll never forget.[11] In fact, I should be able to recite it to little Dave someday, if I feel like it.

Guess I'd better close my station for the night. Darling, don't forget to try and find me some film for my camera. It's a Kodak F/ 8, 40mm.

Good night for now.

Love and kisses,
David

---

[11]   The hardest part of parachuting was landing on the ground. Landing can be difficult depending on the speed and height of the plane. On D-day, a lot of paratroopers received injuries because the C-47s were flying at 150 mph and were a lot closer to the ground than they should have been.

Somewhere in France
June 24, 1944

My Dearest Darling,

Well, you're out of school now. That's great. How does it feel?

I just got news from a church back home where I used to go, that one of my best school chums has been killed in action. I sure hated to hear it. He was in the SP.

So they are praising the paratroops back home, are they? Well, I can say they deserve it and then some. As for me, I'm mystified with my life and body intact.

I hope you're receiving my mail by now. Write as often as you can, darling. Keep that chin up. I'll be back someday.

Forever yours,
David

CHAPTER IV

Red, White, and Blue

We shall not flag or fail. We shall fight in France, we shall fight on the seas and oceans, we shall fight with growing confidence and growing strength in the air, we shall defend our island, whatever the cost may be, we shall fight on the beaches, we shall fight on the landing grounds, we shall fight in the fields and in the streets, we shall fight in the hills; we shall never surrender.

—Winston Churchill,
British prime minister during WWII

Somewhere in France
July 2, 1944

My Dearest Lou,

Just a few lines this evening as it is Sunday and I have a chance to write.

Wish I were back, so I could go to the beach with you this summer. Boy, that would be swell. I can almost relax just thinking about it.

Hope you get your civil service job. It looks like my job is going to hold out for some time. Boy, I wish it were over. But then I'm only one in millions wishing the same.

Yes, Betty Lou, a lot of things have changed in the last few years. But there are a few things that will never change or be forgotten. I'd like to tell you what I got or rather what I had for my birthday. And if I live to be a hundred, I'll never forget that day. I can't tell you the whole story.

But my buddy and I stopped at a French home for some cider, and while drinking that, my partner told them (the French people) of my birthday. They made quite a fuss over it and gave me a bouquet of roses—red, white, and blue—and a big red rose to pin on my jacket. To top all this off, they gave me a bottle of very special wine, which was very good and quite old. It was only about an hour that we spent there. But it will never be forgotten.

Say, this writing paper isn't half bad. It's Jerry's[12] stuff, or used to be. I just took my V-mails out, and every darn one of them is stuck together. I'm having a devil of a time writing this letter. There's a guy in here playing a harp, and I'm trying to drink a cup of coffee and smoke a cigarette. But I'll make it through.

---

12   Jerry was a nickname for Germans during the war.

Well, darling, looks like I'm about out of words. So I'll close for now. Write often. Give my love to the folks.

Forever yours,
David

PS: Don't call me Davie anymore. If you do, I'll get even one of these days. That isn't a threat. Happy, happy.

England
V-Mail
July 12, 1944

My Darling,

Received your letters today. Thanks for the pictures, hon. It's really swell to know you're getting my letters okay.

Gee, it's good to be back here. I can't explain just how good I really feel about it. But so much for that.

Sure hope you get your job, darling. I know it will mean a lot for you to get a good position.

Well, I must close for now. I will try and write a long letter tomorrow. Good night, sweetheart.

Love and kisses,
David

England
August 2, 1944

My Sweetheart,

I hope this finds you okay. I'm fine and in the best of health as yet. Right now, I'm disgusted as hell. Boy, what a damn war this is. Oh well, you wouldn't understand.

Here's hoping you fully recovered by now. I've been wondering about you lately. I know I haven't heard from you in quite awhile. I went for a long walk this evening down by the river or small stream. It's quite beautiful to walk along and just sit on the banks and watch the trout play about. One can turn their mind back to God's country.

While I was there, an old man came up to where I was, and we talked for about two hours, mostly on the contrast of England and the United States. I learned many things of interest about dukes, lords, and earls and of other people of England.

I sure was glad to hear you received my wire, darling. I had a letter from your mother yesterday.

I hope you've got your voice back by now. Say, if I were there, you couldn't argue with me, could you? Ha! Not much anyway. Well, sweetheart, by the grace of God, I'll come through with flying colors and come back to you.

Love always,
David

England
August 28, 1944

My Darling,

Sure glad you went to see the dentist. I had mine checked a few days ago. The doc said I have a swell set, as they all say. I'm going to have them cleaned in a few days though.

During June[13] and part of July, I never brushed my teeth for six weeks, sort of left them out of shape. I lost my toilet kit on D-day. I've got another one now though.

Well, darling, there isn't much to say from this side of the world. The war seems to be going good. But you know as much as I do about that, I guess. I just heard a broadcast from Paris with all the shouting and happiness there seemed to be. I'd like to be there in a way, just for a while in Paris, of course.

Guess I will close now. Write soon, and remember, I love you.

Forever yours,
David

---

[13] June 6, 1944, the day the Allied powers crossed the English Channel and landed on the beaches of Normandy, France, beginning the liberation of Western Europe from Nazi control during World War II. Within three months, the northern part of France would be freed and the invasion force would be preparing to enter Germany, where they would meet up with Soviet forces moving in from the east. D-day—History.com, This Day in History—6/6/1944.

CHAPTER V

WHY WE JUMP

I am a paratrooper.
I hail from every state in the union;
I come from every walk of life.
I hit the silk over every land.

I'm hard and I'm tough—made of the stuff
That asks no quarter, nor gives no quarter,
And take it from me, I NEVER bluff.
I'm briefed and checked while stars look down,
At 2330 I leave the ground.
Two rows of men sit silent then,
Two rows of men on a mission, bent,
Fit and ready—trained to kill.

Two rows of men facing each other,
Husband, son, sweetheart, brother.
Now the takeoff is over, we're in the air,
And what do we think, sitting there!
There's tension in the plane as we fly tonight.
But, thank God it will pass—we know it will pass.

When your belly snaps tight, and the throat goes dry,
And you swallow hard, and you glance at the guy across
And wonder why, all this war, this hell and man-made blight that
ordains somewhere there'll be death tonight.

Then suddenly it comes!

Poised there in the open port door,
Crouched there, leg pulled up,
As you glimpse the stream far below,
Silvery white in the moon's soft glow;
The fields of wheat beside the stream,
Where in days of peace the reapers glean.

As you grab the rip cord, cold and bare,
Catch your breath, leap into space,
A curse on your lips, and a muttered prayer.
Yes, it's then you know and understand;
You're jumping tonight for all mankind,
For every nation, in every home,
For every heart that beats for peace;
And it matters not the creed or race,
It's Congress of Nations jumping through space

To bring to a world the saving grace
Of peace on earth, blessed peace.
Jumping tonight that men may live;
Floating death from out the skies
For anyone who ever tries
To stop this world in it's onward march.
Silent death from out of the blue,
Fighting for peace fighting for you;
Hitting the silk, unafraid,
Sudden death—American made.

—Author unknown

Location Unknown
V-Mail
August 1944

My Dearest Darling,

No letter today, hon. But I had two yesterday, so what can I expect?

Hope this finds you well and happy. I'm okay. So don't worry about me. I wish I had finished high school. But like a young punk, I thought I knew it all. Well, I'll take care of that when I return home. I'm always moving around and getting into something new. It It looks like you'll have quite a job at settling down. Think you can handle it? Ha, I have no doubt.

Remember when you asked me what sort of job I wanted for the future and I wouldn't tell you? The kind of job I would want is only for a single fellow, and I don't want to stay single, not as long as I have you waiting for me.

Well, darling, I must close for now. Write soon and often.

Yours forever.

Love and kisses,
David

Somewhere in France
August 30, 1944

Dear Mother,

Just a few lines tonight as I received three wonderful letters from you today and one from my darling.

It sure was swell to get them. I finally heard from home and, believe me, was I ever glad. Say, you didn't hurt my feelings any about the lighter. If I've said anything that made you think so, I'm sorry. So please forget it.

My grandmother did send me one. I think I told you about it. However, I don't have it now. I lost it and about everything else that I had the night that I jumped, even some pictures of Betty and I. I had them in my field bag and lost the whole damned thing, but that's life. I even lost my Bible, and boy, I could of used it, that is, if I'd had the time. However, I made out as usual.

I want to thank you and Dad for the two very nice cards you sent me. They were swell. By the way, you're the first one to get an airmail letter from me here in France. It seems kind of funny to be writing on this stationery again. But it's much better than V-mail.

You're darn right I'm going to take myself a wife when I get back to Indiana. The only thing that worries me is this army of occupation after the victory is won. I've never spoke to Betty about it, and she probably hasn't even thought about it. But you know as I do that someone is going to have to stay over here, and it's common sense that most of the men who will stay will be young and unmarried. I don't think I have to say anymore about it. If it wasn't for Betty, I wouldn't care. But as it is, I do. I can almost realize how she would probably feel if she saw all the boys coming home and me staying over here another year or so. And in a case like that, a year is a devil of a long time.

Well, Mother, I believe that I've rambled enough for now. I want to write home and also to Betty, so I must close for now.

Give my love to all.

Dave

England
August 31, 1944

My Darling,

It's rather cold here in England today. I guess the fall is really close or perhaps already here.

No letter from you yesterday. So perhaps I'll do better today, huh? I hope so, anyway. I had a letter from a friend of mine here in England. He is in the 8th Air Force.

Darling, don't worry about me, for I'm getting the best care in the world. And the boys in here are really okay. Everyone laughs and jokes in spite of their wounds or hurts. So, again, I say don't worry about me.

Ever hear of a song called "No Letter Today"? Well, I feel like singing it now. But due to the fact that I don't want about 40 size 11 GI shoes flying my way, I won't. I did get a hometown newspaper that was only a month old. Pretty good, huh? My nurse is first class and the best nurse in the ward.

Darn that guy across from me. He keeps whistling a tune I can't place. He doesn't even know what it is and nor does anybody else in here. I'm about to pull my hair out trying to think what it is.

Well, sweetheart, I've raved enough tonight, don't you think? Sure I have. So I'll say good night, sweet dreams, and God bless you. Write soon and often. Oh, just make it every day. I never get tired of them.

Forever yours,
David

PS: Say, do you have some Scotch or Irish in you? I bet you do.

England
September 1944

My Darling Lou,

Well, darling, I received a V-mail in the late mail today.

I have been pretty much in the dumps as I hadn't heard from you for quite awhile. But today, my morale rose to 100 percent.

So you had Labor Day off? You know, I've almost forgotten what our holidays are like even. Oh well, perhaps I can learn to be civilized again someday.

By the way, I heard the other day that some person had suggested passing a bill that would send us tough paratroops to a school in which we are to be taught civilization before returning back home. Ha-ha. That's very thoughtful of them, don't you think? What in the hell do they suppose we are, anyway? Oh, forget it.

No, sweetheart, I never heard of a woman who wasn't full of curiosity, and you're no exception. Ha, just kidding. Darling, I too wish that I could be with you even for a few minutes or so. This war would no doubt seem miles away then.

So you had my football pictures out. Hey, I hope you didn't look holes in them. Gee, I'll have a little recording to do in that parachute album of mine when I get back. I want something to show those five sons of mine. You know, I've almost come to an agreement on that. Okay.

You bet, we'll go over to Chicago and celebrate when I come back. There are some very beautiful places over there.

Well, darling, for tonight it's adios and keep the home fire burning. I'll be back someday soon, I hope.

Forever yours.

Love and kisses,
David

PS: Give Mother, Dad, and the girls my regards.

England
September 3, 1944

My Darling,

No letter today. I wonder how many people say that in a day. Many, no doubt.

I received five hometown papers today, not bad. I still like to read them though. I also received a box of Martha Washington candy from a friend back home. Yum, yum.

Darling, where this poem came from, I don't know. But I liked it so well, and it has such a meaning that I thought I would send it to you.

Forever yours,
Dave

> You are lonely there without me
> As I am lonely for you here
> I long to be back with folks
> And the sweetheart I hold so dear
>
> So my dear one you must have courage
> And help to get this great battle won
> So then I can come back to you
> And then our hearts will beat as one
>
> So I'll be waiting for you Darling
> Waiting when the war is won
> Then we will live our lives together
> And we will never part, no never more
>
> —Author unknown

CHAPTER VI

STRONG HAND OVER ME

Now the trumpet summons us again—not as a call to bear arms, though arms we need; not as a call to battle, though embattled we are; but a call to bear the burden of a long twilight struggle, year in and year out, "rejoicing in hope, patient in tribulation," a struggle against the common enemies of man; tyranny, poverty, disease and war itself.

—John F. Kennedy, thirty-fifth
president of the United States

England
September 4, 1944

My Darling,

I just listened to the news. It sounds good to me. But the war isn't won yet. Oh no, I think some people have their hopes up too much. It's nice to think so though.

What's wrong, darling? You haven't written so much lately. I know I don't write very often. But if you were in my place, I'm afraid you wouldn't either.

So you have my picture on your desk at work? The town where that was taken is quite an historical place with lots of caves there. The song "Rock of Ages" was written there, or so I'm told.

Well, I guess this is Labor Day back in those United States. Are they celebrating? Oh, for the times we used to spend on Labor Day—fairs, picnics, etc. Do you realize that it will soon be a year since we have seen each other? We'll see each other before the year is up. But I doubt it. Encouraging, aren't I?

Some babe is singing "Don't Sweetheart Me," and boy is she murdering it. I could do better even. And what a disgrace that would be.

Please don't worry about me. I have a strong hand over me.

Yours forever,
David

England
September 15, 1944

My Darling,

Just a few lines today as I haven't written to you for several days now. I probably won't hear from you for days and perhaps weeks now, but so much for that.

Remember my friend Johnny Kiewicz? Well, he plans to be married upon his return home, and of course, we are invited. I'm sort of supposed to stand up for him or something. Anyway, there's a great celebration planned. Perhaps it's planning a little far ahead. But I told him I didn't think so and that it was something to look forward to. It's a Polish wedding, and if you know anything about them, then you know what they're like. I've never been to one. But I've heard plenty about them.

Will write when I hear from you as it's much easier to write when you receive mail. Of course, you know that as well as I do. So for now, I will close.

Forever yours.

With all my love,
David

England
September 27, 1944

My Darling,

Well, here I am again or, as the saying goes, here's that man again.

Hope this finds you and the folks well. Soon, it will be two weeks since now since I've had a letter from you. It will probably be a month now before my mail catches up with me.

As you'll notice darling, I'm in the hospital.[14] So naturally, you'll want to know why. Well, I've been to Holland, and up there, I had a little trouble and got careless, I guess. I always said that only the careless get hurt. But don't worry, kiddo. I'll be back in there pitching soon.

Are you still holding down that good job you had? I hope so. I'll walk in some afternoon and take you home, that is, if you keep the job for a year or so.

Have you heard from my folks lately, for I think grandma would of let you know about me? I'm sure they must know about me by now.

I'm getting the best of care. It's really nice here in the ward. All the boys are okay. The nurses are swell. In fact, that just makes everything okay.

Forever yours,
David

---

[14]   Dad caught a bullet in his leg and had surgery for his kneecap many years later.

England
September 29, 1944

My Sweetheart,

No, love, no nothing but memories. Say, what am I complaining about? Those memories are the most wonderful things of my life. I live them over a thousand times a day. Yes, and then some.

You know, darling, I'll never forget when you said, "And you'll come back." I've often thought of that when death seemed so [censored] near. Then I'd say a little prayer, and usually everything would come out all right. I remember after I was hit, the chaplin told me to say a prayer and that sometimes it would help. He's right. It does help.

I received my Purple Heart today. It's really a beautiful medal. I pray to God that I may never receive a cluster for it.[15] I'll be sending it home soon. Do you ever worry about our future? I do.

I have a couple of your pictures on the little desk at my bedside. One is of us when I was home on furlough. The other has long been my favorite. It's very small, and you were about 16 years old at the time it was taken. You have a white blouse and a white flower in your hair. Do you remember it? Of course, that wonderful smile and the little dimple catch the eye.

Well, darling, I guess I'd better close for tonight. Oh, by the way, little David is still with me. I almost lost him this time, but

---

[15] Dad was praying that he never receive a Cluster as that would mean another injury. Dad, in fact, went on to receive that Cluster for his Purple Heart in the Battle of the Bulge. In US Military, Oak Leaf Clusters on ANY medal indicate multiple awards of that medal.

I didn't. So I'll bring him home safe. Then of course, we'll do something about the real one after time.

Goodnight, my darling. Sweet dreams.

All my love.

Forever yours,
David

England
September 30, 1944

My Darling,

Another month has gone by now and marks well over a year that I've been in the troops and something like ten months since I've seen you. Let's hope and pray that it will not be that much longer.

The chaplin was in this morning, and he talked to me for a long time. It was really good to talk to him, not just religion, but of current events and everything in general.

Well, darling, it's late in the evening and Saturday night too. Oh, what I can't think of for tonight, a little girl back in Indiana, many meters away.

Holy smokes, there's a new copy of *Yank*[16] floating around. We're almost fighting over it, so time out.

Back again. Everything's okay, that is, except Sad Sack and a few GIs with their usual gripes.

Signing off for tonight, darling.

Lots of love and kisses.

Forever yours,
David

---

[16] *Yank*, the army weekly, was one of the finest military publications of World War II. Yank, The Army Weekly: World War Two Magazine | Writinghood.

England
October 4, 1944

Just a few words this evening. I'm not feeling so hot today. Tomorrow I'll be okay again.

No letter today. I should be getting some soon. It should not take more than two weeks. God, I hope it comes soon. That's about all one lives for here. That's easy to understand.

Boy would I like to be back in the states now. I'd like to take in a couple of good football games and God knows what else. I'm afraid the little woman just couldn't hold me. And then, maybe she could. One never knows.

I'll be glad when those pictures arrive. I've lost everything except a few small snap shots, which happened to be on me. What a world.

I haven't told you anything about Holland, have I, darling? No one ever said I couldn't. But anyway, there isn't much to say. As you know, the country has many canals, dikes, and etc.

I stood in the door of the plane as we flew over a lot of this and had a wonderful view, little farms and network of roads below with people looking up into the sky with awe.

I'll tell you a real story about it someday. There's a nice story in that trip.

Love and kisses,
David

England
October 9, 1944

My Darling,

Another week has started to roll by now. Yesterday it was Sunday. It was very quiet and peaceful and very lonesome too. Wish you could have had a little visit with me. That would have been like a star from heaven.

I received your letter of September 27th darling. It was swell. It was almost like hearing you talk. I'm feeling much better today and getting along swell. So don't worry. I'll get along as long as I receive those reports from you every day or so.

Yes, darling, you're eighteen now. I think no one realizes that more than I do. I will never forget where I was on your eighteenth birthday, September 24th.[17]

You bet I'm glad to hear you are working with your father, darling. And why shouldn't you be, as I don't like for my future wife to be working just anywhere. Darling, I'll be glad when I return and we can be married and start that little family we want so much. But let's not be sure of a fast return on my part. I won't express my opinion on when I'll get back. I assure you, it will be some time.

Betty Lou, you won't regret giving blood to the blood bank. If you could only realize what it means to donate blood for the wounded on the battlefield. I know that it saved many a life.

---

[17] Operation Market-Garden was conducted September 17-25, 1944, in an attempt to capture bridges over the Rhine. Operation Market-Garden—Operation Market Garden 1944.

Well, sweetheart, I must close for now. Write often, Lou darling.
Say hello to everyone for me.

Lots of love and kisses.

Forever yours,
David

Location Unknown
V-Mail
November 6, 1944

My Darling,

Sorry, it's been some time now since I've written to you. I'm afraid you'll have to get used to it for a while now. I'll write as often as possible.

Hope you have received my letter telling you that I was out of the hospital. My wound has healed up very good, and I'm active once more. And that means a lot. I hate hospitals. They treat you swell though.

Well, darling, my mail is catching up. I received twenty-three letters today. I'm only writing a V-mail now. I'll try and write a long airmail tomorrow.

Love and kisses,
David

Location Unknown
November 8, 1944

My Darling,

Here comes a letter. Please excuse the pencil. I probably hate writing with it as much as you would. But we don't always have what we want, do we?

Don't worry about me, Betty. I'm quite well, so the doctors say. I'm ready to agree with them. It's good to know that I have pictures on the way. I haven't received any of them yet. I went to see *The Story of Dr. Wassell* the other day. It was pretty good, that is what I saw of it. I left before it had hardly started. It just didn't agree with me somehow.

Yes, darling, time drags, but then the future is going to pass a hell of a lot slower. I mean the next year or so. Every day will seem like a lifetime. Ha. Why ask me whether I like to see women wear slacks without a girdle? How would I know? We'll have no remarks about that either.

Listen, darling, it's ever so good to hear you say you'll be waiting for me no matter what happens. As of now, I'm okay. I mean, I'm not disabled or anything. But this war isn't over yet. Anyway, I'll be seeing more action. I wouldn't get out even if I could now. There's something deeper than you'll ever feel. What I started to say was this. There are a hell of a lot of lads that are coming back without limbs, blind and every other way. Their sweethearts and wives will stick with them either because they really love them or just feel sorry. I know that I could never marry a girl who just felt sorry for me. You'll probably never know what I'm talking about unless you know of a case. I do. Well, but enough of that.

Whatever happens, Lou, remember I love you way down deep. There have been times when I thought I'd never see you or anyone back there. But now a rest with a look at your picture with old memories and just knowing you're waiting for me. I can't afford not to come back. Do you understand what I mean, darling?

Well, it's getting rather cold over here now, hon. But don't worry. I'll keep dressed warm. I'm a soldier of the best-dressed army in the world. Just remember that.

I must close, darling. Write soon and often. I'll write when I can. Give my love to mother and dad.

Always yours,
David

England
November 12, 1944

Hello Mother,

Just a few lines as it's been some time since I've written to you. I just don't write very much at all. I hope Betty isn't angry with me. But I'm afraid I couldn't explain to her if I tried.

I went to see the movie *Home in Indiana* last night. Gee, but it was good. I used to go to those races every summer. Hope this finds everyone well and happy. I'm getting along swell except for the fact that I'm bothered with headaches now and then, nothing serious though.

Well, Mother, it's another Christmas at war, at least, it looks like that now. Perhaps next year will see the world at peace. I hope so, but it's better to fight this one to the finish than to have my son fighting another war. My age and the age of thousands of other boys are today is the best part of our lives.

Sometimes all of this seems like one big dream to me. It just doesn't seem possible that I've been in France and Holland and what I've seen and that I'm still alive and well. But I am, and I thank God for that. I've got a lot to come back to, Mother. That's why I'll get back because I believe in her love for me. If she should ever let me down, well, I just don't have words for it. I guess you understand though. That is the best part of writing to you because you understand what I am trying to say.

Well, I suppose I've said about enough. Anyway, I've got to get a letter off to your little daughter. Give my regards to Dad and all.

Lots of love,
David

England
November 13, 1944

My Darling,

Just had a Coke. Yes, that's right. And now I'm sitting in front of the best fireplace in the whole world. I've also got one of those big soft easy chairs that a soldier dreams of. But I'm not dreaming, hon. Gee, but this fire is nice. Wish you were with me. But then, I wouldn't be writing this letter. I'm really getting a rest now, and I do need it, if I may say so. I will tell you about it someday.

There's some swell music playing on the wireless. Would you like to dance? Let's just sit this one out. It's rather cold out tonight, not too much though, just enough to make one feel good. It's warm enough in here to make one sleepy. (Time out while I go to a show, sweetheart).

Back again. I saw *Hitler's Gang*. You've probably seen it. It's pretty crude, but every little part is easy to believe. Gee, hon, I'm getting sleepy, and I'm not kidding. You don't mind, do you?

Hope you like the picture I sent you yesterday, darling. Everyone around here says it doesn't look like me. So if you think I look thin and a little serious, don't worry about it.

Must close for tonight, my darling. Please write as often as you possibly can. Say hello to the folks for me.

Forever yours,
David

England
November 18, 1944

My Darling,

Gee, it's ages since I've heard from you. At least, it seems so. Guess when I don't hear from you for a couple of days, I don't seem to be able to take it, but that's life in the army.

Still haven't received the pictures you sent. Wish they would come soon, for I'll probably miss them if they don't. I have been reading *One World* by Wendell L. Willkie. What I've read is very good. Have you read it? I used to read a lot. But since I've left the Air Force, I've done very little of it. One just doesn't have the time for it even though they want to.

I've been listening to what seems to be a trail of Hitler and all his men. What they don't put on the radio these days. Most of it, I can't see.

I went to Cardiff the other day, which is in South Wales. I know some people out there. Their son was in the Merchant Navy in the worst days. Anyway, they've been very good to me. These people are Welsh, and they treated me to a swell Welsh dinner. The best dish was rabbit, fixed up in their own style, of course—first I'd ever eaten anything like it.

While I was there, their son Jim took me around to all the interesting places, like the civic center. They have some really beautiful buildings there and an old castle. I only saw this from the outside. But it was quite large, with huge walls around it. I wish you could see some of these places. I know you've seen pictures and paintings. But that is not like really seeing them.

Well, Betty, I've raved about nothing long enough. Write often.

I'm forever yours,
David

England
November 23, 1944

My Darling,

You'll have to excuse the pencil, hon. It's the best I can do. But then many great and important letters have been written in pencil, so why not mine? It may not be great, but it's darn important.

Thanksgiving Day. Yes, it'll soon be a year since we said good-bye. I was at a parade this time last year, feeling pretty proud. I still am, and why not? I had plenty to be proud of then and even more now.

I've had a pretty swell day, darling. We had turkey for dinner with several of the trimmings, even pumpkin pie, which wasn't bad. It would have been much better at home though.

Have you received the photo I sent you? It's not very good. I have some more coming, which I hope will be better. Hope they're in time for Christmas; that's what they were made for.

I saw two pictures today, one was a navy film and the other one was Buffalo Bill. I didn't really like either of them. But then, I guess I'm rather hard to please. Do you think so? Never mind answering that.

Sometimes I wish we were already married, darling. Perhaps there would have been a little one by now. Nothing could make me any happier. But I guess it's best this way. At least you don't have so many worries. You're still the only one, Betty Lou. I've never met anyone who could take your place. Darling, you need never worry. You are my whole life.

It's raining out, Lou. It's pattering on the roof. Do you remember the night we took your father's car and went for a drive? Gee, but it was raining really hard that night. I just changed from writing in pencil to a pen. I just got this pen from Fritz, a pal of mine. I could have been writing with it the whole time.

Well, darling, it's time to leave you tonight. Do write often and keep the home fires burning bright. Cheerio for now. Give my regards to the folks.

Forever yours.

Love,
David

Location Unknown
December 7, 1944

> *Let me tell you my little tale,*
> *It's very sad you'll probably say,*
> *No heed to my gripes*
> *And pains. I really can't*
> *Complain.*
>   —Author unknown

Dear Betty,

It's been a long time since I've written to you, and it's been about three weeks since I've heard from you. But it's probably being held up somewhere.

Hope this finds you and your folks well and in the best of health. I'm about the same. So I guess I won't complain.

I don't know whether I'll ever jump again or not. Sometimes I think it would be best. But as long as the war goes on, I don't want to be in any other branch of service. I think you understand that.'

Must close for now. Write when you can.

Love,
David

CHAPTER VII

SOMEWHERE IN FRANCE

It is a fearful thing to lead this great peaceful people into war, into the most terrible and disastrous of all wars, civilization itself seeming to be in the balance. But the right is more precious than peace, and we shall fight for the things which we have always carried nearest our hearts—
for Democracy.

—Woodrow Wilson, twenty-eighth
president of the United States

France
December 11, 1944

Hello Mother,

Gee, but it's been ages since I've written to you. I hope I'm not in trouble when I get back home.

I received your letter of November 21st, and it sure was a swell letter too. Besides Lou, I'd rather hear from you than anyone else I know of. So just remember that you are second on my list even if I don't write real often. You write me about so many things of interest that Betty doesn't mention.

Say, Mom, you hit the nail on the head when you spoke of Lou's dimples. I often think about them, and every time I look at her pictures (which is quite often), I think of them. Yes, she's really cute when she shows those. I hope she never loses them.

Yes, I hope Lou forgets the acting, and I think she will after I come home—at least, I hope so. I'm sure she has the talent, but show people are seldom happy—at least, that is my experience.

None of the packages have arrived as yet, but they should any day, I hope so, anyway. I'd sure like to see the house now. I'll bet it's swell; if it can be made that way, then Dad can do it.

Well, Mother Livingston, don't worry about me. I'm okay. I'm back in France for now. It's not so bad over here. I can think of lots of other places much worse. Then again, those United States are wonderful.

Must close for now. Say hello to Lou's sisters, Barbara and Virginia, and Dad for me. Write when you can and give my love to Betty.

David

Somewhere in France
December 1944

My Darling,

After three weeks, I finally received three wonderful letters from you, hon—one from mother, three from home, and a couple of others. Gee, but it was good to get some mail.

Say, I'd like to see little Joe. I'll bet he's a sweet little fellow. I'm glad he's good company for you. I wish a thousand times we had one of our own. But wishing does no good. It makes my life easier though when I think of you and things like that. Someday our dreams and plans will come true. This war can't last forever, you know. But it can last a hell of a long time.

Darling, I know I haven't been writing very much lately. But I hope you understand. As you've probably noticed, I'm back with my outfit now. Gee, it was good to see all of the boys again.

Betty Lou, I could have gotten out of the parachute troops if I had wanted to. But, darling, it's like I said before: I went into combat with them, and I'd rather see the war through with them. When you come right down on the line, this is a swell brand of the service. I know a lot of people don't like us. They talk about us and call us killers and God knows what just because we raise a little hell now and then. But they think the world of us when we're giving the enemy the once over. Boy, could I write a letter about some of those cocky civilians back there. But I won't as it probably won't get past the censor[18] if I wrote what things I could think of.

---

[18] In WW2, newspapers and television news were censored. Censorship is when the government decides what or what not to show the people. Government considered it necessary in order to boost morale, but it was also a dangerous precedent because it violated 1st Amendment free speech. The trend of censorship has

You asked about my wound. Well, guess I can tell you. It's pretty well healed up now. It's right below my left knee running down the outside of my leg and about six inches long. I also injured my kneecap. Remember, I hurt it on the jump before. But outside of that, I'm pretty healthy. I'm sending you some pictures. I hope you like them. The boys say they're not like me at all. It's been one year this week since you last saw me. I've changed some, not in my features, but inside. Well, so much for that, darling.

You said something about not being able to buy more bonds. I know you and your folks are buying the limit. But, darling, there are thousands who are not. They say they simply can't do it. They can if only they would stop and think of the American boys who are giving their very lives for them. These lads can't buy another life. When they hear of a big victory, thousands of Germans killed and taken prisoner, I often wonder if they stop and think of their own lads who are also lying on the battlefields. Hell no, they don't, not one in a thousand, not even some of the people I know from my end of the state. Oh, I could blow my top all day, darling. But I won't bore you with it.

Look, sweetheart, if your cooking is bad, I'll raise the devil. Ha. Then again, I'd probably smile and force it down and say it was swell. I'm not worried about it though. Yes, I've been told many times you look like Simone Simon. But I'll be damned if I can see it.

Darling, you were talking about a girl coming to live at your home with the family. If you like her and she's a good girl, she'll make a good pal for you, and besides, you'd be doing a big favor to her. But that's none of my concern of course.

Well, darling, I must close. Please write often. Until we meet again.

Forever yours,
David

---

been a common theme in wars throughout America and across the world and is a dangerous side effect for war.

France
December 16, 1944

My Darling,

It's Saturday night, and it finds me here in the camp. You may not believe it. But over here, it's the best place to be.

There are good programs on the radio tonight and a good fire, comfortable enough for a king. I received a letter from you today, hon. Gee, but it was good to hear from you again. It took sixteen days to get here.

I guess I'll sleep late in the morning. Sunday is the only time you ever get to do that. Boy, how I wait for the day when no sergeant will blow his brains out on a whistle, trying to get me up. Don't you ever try that because, darling, it just won't work.

It's good to hear that you went to a party. Perhaps we can go to a few when I come home. We've missed all the things like that, and it hurts. But we'll make up for it. I want to go to Paris one of these days, whether I get to or not is something else, I guess.

Must close now, darling. Hope you don't mind two letters in one envelope. Write often, Lou.

Forever yours,
David

CHAPTER VIII

A Time to Remember

In honor of the Battered Bastards of Bastogne.

Let us pause and reflect
On a battle we'll never forget . . .
'Twas December of 44,
All our troopers were at war . . .
Tested on Overlord and MarketGarden, Screaming Eagles
tone and hardened. Fought their way to the Ardennes, Never
pausing to take a rest . . . Knocking hard on Hitler's gate,
Paratroopers would seal his fate . . . 'Twas their job to protect,
Bastogne's borders from conquest . . . German armies had
amassed, This breakthrough would be the last . . . To reach
the Meuse, to tighten the noose, To strangle the allies on the
loose . . . Artillery pounded day and night, All of Belgium
shook with fright . . . 'Twas a mistake, the Germans thought,
Defending Bastogne, all would be lost . . . "Send the message,"
their General said, "surrender now or you'll be dead . . ." The
101st don't have a chance, All will die by the Nazi lance . . .

Fighting sleep and the bitter cold, The 101st would surely fold . . . Low on supplies and fighting ammunition, They'd surrender without condition . . . The only thing he didn't consider, Screaming Eagles would not wither . . . Airborne soldiers tried and tested, Their fighting spirit would not be bested . . . General McAuliffe said one work, They wouldn't believe what they heard . . . What is this, "NUTS," he said, The Germans answered with armor and lead . . . Artillery and armor, shells were cracking, Nazi Infantry were attacking . . . Airborne courage was not lacking, They'd fight like hell and wait for backing . . . Holding on to precious ground, Inflicting damage with every round . . . Airborne soldiers ought and bled, Winter's snow was turning red . . . "The Battered Bastards of Bastogne" fought like Belgium was their own . . . Hold on they did, to turn the tide, To attack when Patton arrived . . . Allied armor to lend a hand, They chased the Nazi's to Rhineland . . . Fighting hard as they went, Their Airborne spirit would not relent . . . Fifty years have come and gone, Time can't diminish what they have done . . . "The Battle of the Bulge" was a hard fought one, Belgium was free and the war was won . . . These Paratroopers of World War II, Fought like hell and saw it through . . . Screaming Eagles who fought and bled, Their fighting spirit will never be dead . . . Let us pause and reflect, To give them honor and respect . . . Our fallen brothers, we'll never forget, Their sacrifices are part of us yet . . . Many crosses stand as a reminder, Airborne soldiers have never been finer . . . Screaming Eagles proud and true, Defending freedom for me and you . . . God bless them all, for what they've done, Airborne heroes, everyone . . . Hitler is finished, the world is free, Let's celebrate the victory . . . !
God Bless You All,

Airborne . . . !

—Peter S. Griffin

Somewhere in France
December 17, 1944

My Darling,

It's Sunday evening and no letter today. I received a package from your folks. Give them my thanks. It arrived okay, and the popcorn did the trick.

I'm smoking an English cigarette, and it stinks. I've been smoking everything but dried leaves. I guess I'd smoke that too if they were dry. Boy, I think the cigarette deal stinks, and I don't mean maybe. When a soldier can't have what he needs to smoke, there's something crooked in the deal. Well, so much for that. It's no use complaining to you about it.

Wish those pictures of you would hurry up and come. It seems like it's been months since you sent them.

Think I will close for now because I feel like the devil and will go to bed.

Write often, darling.

All my love,
David

Western Front
December 28, 1944

My Darling,

Another year will soon be gone. As I write you this letter, I'm drinking a cup of coffee, real honest stuff. And does it ever taste good.

For days, our food has been very slim, and at times, we have lived off the land. It is much better now though.

One of these days, you will probably read about where I'm at and what my division has done.

Hope you had a nice Christmas, darling. It wasn't so nice up here. Jerry was up real early on Christmas morning. I think I got the biggest scare so far that day. I shall never forget the smell of pines as it will remind me of this war.[19] So that's one Christmas I shall never forget, but enough for this end of the road.

---

[19]   Christmas Day 1944 was a horrendous day for the 502, 401 & 463 filled with see saw battle overcoming serious odds to keep the Germans from getting into Bastogne. This was one of the hardest fought battles of the siege. Dad was always sad around Christmas. We thought it was because his mother passed away around the holidays. But upon reading his letters, we discovered that Christmas in particular was a somber time for him for many reasons. But this did not deter him from giving us a fresh-cut pine tree every year.

Leo Barron and Don Cygan give a compelling and detailed account of the Five-O-Deuce's gallant and unrelenting defense of Champs and Rolle that Christmas in 1944 in the book, "NO SILENT NIGHT."

We still have a lot of snow up here, and today, it's cloudy and looks like it might snow some more. I hope not. It's miserable enough as it is. It's cold and foggy as heck sometimes.

Don't worry about me, honey. I'm feeling pretty good except for my leg. It hurts at times. But there's no use complaining about it.

I noticed a Christmas tree the other day, darling. A civilian family had it with trimmings and things like we have at home. Of course, I didn't see any presents lying around. I only saw it through a window. But there probably wasn't any.

Well, sweetheart, I must close now. Write often, and remember, I love you very much.

Forever yours,
David

Belgium
V-Mail
December 29, 1944

My Darling,

My first mail in two weeks arrived today. I don't think I've ever been happier at receiving mail. I had two from you, one from your mother, and one from home.

I was glad to hear that your mother went to visit my folks while she was down in the section. My Grandmother Amelia liked her very much.

I'll bet my brothers and sisters were tickled to death when they received their presents from you, darling. Thanks a million!

For now I must close, hon. I'll write every chance I get. Say hello to the folks for me. All my love.

Forever yours,
David

Belgium
V-Mail
December 30, 1944

My Darling,

Just a few lines tonight before I take my shift on the radio.

Received a swell card from Virginia and Barb today. Give them many thanks for me. They are swell kids. But then the whole darn family is as far as I'm concerned.

It's snowing again tonight; no moon like there has been the past few nights, but still, you can't complain because you can see pretty good.

I guess you know just about where I'm at now because I heard a news broadcast today, and they spoke of my division. Had a news correspondent take my name, city, and state yesterday and a couple of other things that weren't really made that clear to me—at least, I won't mention it just now but will later when I get the real dope on it.

Must close for now. Write often, darling. A letter from you is worth more than anything else.

All my love,
David

Belgium
V-Mail
December 31, 1944

My Darling,

It's the end of the year, and instead of the usual celebration, I'm sitting up here in a snow-covered country, and it's still snowing.

No mail from you in a couple of days now. Of course, I don't expect it, but it is something to look forward to. Just had a couple of shots of brandy, kind of warms you up, really hits the spot up here, and no more than that doesn't hurt.

Sure hope those pictures hurry up and get here. Kind of hate to get them up here though because I couldn't very well take care of them. God knows when those packages will get to me, probably by next Christmas, I guess.

So long for now, darling. Write often and say hello to the folks for me.

All my love,
David

Belgium
V-mail
January 2, 1945

My Darling,

Guess you know where I'm at by now. That is, if you've been reading the papers and listening to the news. I'll bet your father has been following the news pretty close.

Oh, how I'd love to be a sailor and sail the deep blue sea. If our son ever goes to war, sweetheart (and I pray he never does), he'll be a sailor boy.

Good night, my darling. Say a little prayer for me. Write often.

All my love,
David

V-mail[20]
January 4, 1945
Belgium

My Darling,

I received four more letters from you today, with the most recent from December 26th.

It would be nice here for a sleigh ride if this were a peaceful country. The scenery is really beautiful. But as usual, the marks of war are all around.

I must close now.

All my love,
David

---

[20] The V-mail system, named after the WWII "V for *victory*" symbol, was developed to help reduce the shipping space needed for the massive increase in mail being sent between American armed forces overseas and their family and friends at home. Victory Mail of the Second World War | A Continuous Lean.

The letters dated January 2, 3, 4, 5, 7 & 22nd of 1945 were originally found with 1944 dates but corrected to avoid confusion in the timeline & proper sequence. Dad was recovering from a shell shock injury in The Battle of the Bulge in December 1944 & in his confusion continued to write 1944, when it was really 1945 . . .

January 4, 1945
Belgium

My Darling,

You're doing okay, kid, as long as I get mail like I have in the last few days, five letters in about two days—not bad at all. Boy, I can stand plenty of them right now.

It's still the same old story up here on the front, darling, cold and snowing. However, I'm inside most of the time. Right now, I'm operating the radio, as I was the other night when I wrote you.

You bet little Dave[21] is still with me, darling, and he's really been around and through plenty. I pray that the real one will never see that day. And it won't be necessary if the American people do as they should and not be so damn soft. I wish they would let the soldiers handle the problem.

So one of the steel mills is on strike? What do they want now, eggs in their beer?[22] Also I wish they would let us deal with that. Our industry has and is doing a great job. But I can't see why they ever strike. It's a damn cinch, we can't out here. You lose your life if you let down your guard here. I must close for now.

Always yours,
David

---

[21] Little Dave, or Davey, mentioned throughout is a reference to a son he hopes to have one day.

[22] A bonus, something for nothing, as in "What do you want—egg in your beer?" This expression dates from about 1940 and became widespread during World War II. The origin is unknown since adding egg to beer does not improve the taste. What does "egg in your beer" mean? | "egg in your beer" meaning.

Belgium
V-mail
January 5, 1945

My Darling,

I still have about an hour of my shift left tonight so will send off another V-mail.

So you don't think the people at home are suffering much? Listen, darling, they don't a damn bit. They've got better jobs than they ever had. They're spending more money than ever. Their homes aren't being shelled or bombed. Yes, it must be terrible for some of them.

The only ones that are hurt back there are the people who have lost their sons and loved ones in this fight for freedom. Hell, most people think we're fighting for someone else. Maybe so, but in order to keep our government and way of life, we too must be in it.

I wonder if you really understand. Must close. Write often.

Love,
David

Belgium
January 7, 1945

My Darling,

So the Four-Fs[23] scramble for war jobs after the mobilization proposal? How does that sound to you? To me it sounds lousy. But no doubt it is true. For I know several men who should be in the army and aren't.

Hell, if I were in the States, I'd be in a lower class than four F. Yet those lousy good-for-nothings are running free. Oh well, why talk about something like that? But honest, it burns me up.

I'm a lucky guy to have someone as nice as you to come home to. It's just getting home is my problem. But I'll get there no matter how long it takes. I'm on the radio now.

Darling, it's twelve o'clock. Gee, I'm kind of sleepy. But I've got two more hours to pull. It isn't so bad though. It's inside. The only worry you have is when Jerry throws a few shells over.

Darling, did you ever sit and watch the flames in a fire? I do quite often. I did tonight before coming on duty. It takes my mind away from everything around me. It seems I can see so many things as the logs burn away. Well, maybe you think it's crazy. But when I have my own home, I'm going to have a nice fireplace.

Darling, I'm sure you've been reading the news lately. No doubt you've been reading about my outfit and didn't know it. I'm in

---

23 A 4F was a draft classification that meant medically unfit to serve. What did a 4H military rating mean in World War 2?—Yahoo.

the First Allied Airborne Army[24] and went out of the Airborne Division. I don't think I told you that.

Well, Lou, I must close for now. Write soon and often.

Forever yours,
David

---

[24] *First Allied Airborne Army.* During its eight-month existence, the First Allied Airborne Army would execute two large-scale airborne assaults, Operation MARKET and Operation VARSITY. An important addition to the SHAEF forces came from the establishment of the First Allied Airborne Army in August 1944. The First Allied Airborne Army was formed as a major command operationally subordinate to SHAEF and not under an army group. The Airborne Army was established to coordinate the air and ground forces required for airborne operations. To assist in the conduct of airborne operations and to simplify command difficulties, the Airborne Army was an integrated US-British headquarters.

First Allied Airborne Army—GlobalSecurity.org—Reliable.

American Red Cross Hospital
January 15, 1945

My Darling,

It's been a while since I've written to you. But I've been on the move. I'll try and catch up on it.

I guess this hospital is where I make my home for a while, not too long I hope. Sure is cold around here, but not like it was up on the front. I'm now in a place I was seven months ago. There's not much to write about, darling.

There was an odd occurrence though on the ambulance as I came in last night. The four patients and the driver were all from Indiana and from the southern part too. The driver lived only a little way from my hometown and knew some of the people I know. It was a rowdy bunch of Hoosiers though.[25]

Above my head here in the ward is a loudspeaker. The news comes on and makes it nice. The news was good today and so was dinner. Darling, when you write, just continue to write to my old outfit.

I'll probably be back before long, and it would just take longer to catch up with me if you wrote to this address. I'll write the mail orderly and have him send my mail to me. Write often. Enclosed is a small article for you to save, darling.

Forever yours,
David

---

[25] Dad was a Hoosier and country boy from southern Indiana.

France
American Red Cross Hospital
January 16, 1945

My Darling,

Another day has passed away. The news is good from all over the world.

It's Sunday, and I saw a GI show today. It was called *Sweat It Out*. I thought it was good. There was one part I wish everybody could see and hear.

The play was a one-man act. This man had been killed, and he told what he had died for. I won't try to tell you what it was like. You wouldn't understand, no one back there would.

I wonder when I'll get some mail. I sure hope it isn't too long. There is a swell program on the radio now. It's the *GI Journal*. It provides a few good laughs anyway.

I've been reading the story of Dr. Wassell today. I saw the picture in England called "One World." But there is a difference in the book.

The nurse just gave me a shot. She was gentle. But the stuff in that needle packs a hit. Guess I better close, Lou.

I've made enough mistakes for a dozen letters. Please excuse them.

Love,
David

Somewhere in France
American Red Cross
January 1945

My Dearest Lou,

I saw a film tonight; *Marriage Is a Private Affair* was the name of it. I guess it was a good example of many wartime marriages, having no experience, I wouldn't know.

It was beautiful out this afternoon. But it's now snowing like heck and just as cold. I'd hate to be in a foxhole tonight, but a lot of poor devils are. I feel for them on a night like this. Guess I'll be back soon myself. It looks like it anyway. I'm as well as I'll ever be I guess.

Gee, but that little baby was cute in the show tonight, a little boy. Sometimes, I wish I had a couple like that. Then again, I'm thankful I haven't yet. I'd like to know my boy and have him know me as he grows up. I guess you learn a lot when you're out in the world and see the misery that is in it. You have no idea. I pray to God that you may never have to realize it. You can read those things for days and weeks. But you don't really know. When I come home, darling, you may not believe everything I tell you. Of course, if you don't believe the things I tell you, I'm going to be angry. Oh, by now I probably have you very mixed up by now, so I'll shut up.

I have just listened to a news report. It sounded very good, but it's too good to last for very long. By that I mean the hardest is yet to come.

Must close for tonight, darling.

All my love,
David

American Red Cross Hospital
France
January 22, 1945

My Darling,

Just a few words to let you know I'm okay. Hope this letter finds you the same.

I saw the picture film *Up in Arms* today. It only made me realize how little time we have had together and how little we really know each other. It was rather a silly film. It seems like everything I see or read takes me along that road.

I hope to be leaving here soon and go back to my outfit. At least I'll get some mail when I get back up there anyway and that's something.

The old tanker next to me here is making some sort of a carpet. I kid him all the time about it. But it's turning out pretty nice. I made a cover for my camera and laced it up pretty nice.

Darling, let me know if you're receiving the clippings and other little things I happen to send home.

Forever yours,
David

France
American Red Cross Hospital
January 24, 1945

My Darling,

I'm happy tonight. Do you mind? It's thousands of miles from you, and I can say that just knowing that I have you helps me. Perhaps I'm a little drunk on love tonight.

I just came from the show *It Happened Tomorrow*, crazy but good. After seeing the picture, I decided I didn't want to know anything about the future.

It's beautiful out tonight, a little hazy with almost a full moon. Would be a good night for a drive. How about that? Would you like that? And on the way home, we'd stop at one of our small places for something to eat.

The nurse just came in making her rounds. She asked if everyone was happy. I spoke for all. Of course, I don't think she believed me, not that I blame her.

There's plenty of discussion today about everything in general, one being about the women, which of course is always high on the list. We were talking about whether most of them would want to leave their jobs after the war. I didn't set in on that one.

It looks like I'll reach twenty-one before I return doesn't it? They say life begins at forty. But I'm going to make the best out of the next twenty years with family life, you bet.

I'm being a little more serious, darling. What do you think of my going to school after I come home? Do you like the idea or not?

Perhaps I should wait until I get back there before talking about it even or never, who knows.

Good night for now.

All my love,
David

France
January 25, 1945

My Dearest,

I'm doing better these days. I'm at a desk or riding a jeep, so that's not hard on me is it?

As long as I'm not around any gunfire or explosions, I do okay. Otherwise, I get nervous as heck and just about go nuts. I haven't told you before, but the real reason I was sent to the hospital from Bastogne was the fact that I was shell-shocked. On Christmas morning, a shell came through the roof of the house I was operating my radio in. It tore up my radio and threw shrapnel all over the room, leaving about a three-foot hole in the roof. But not one little piece touched me.

However, the explosion set off my already tensed nerves, and I just damn near went nuts, not right away though but in the days that followed. I did fall and injure my leg also. I was really a wreck when I went to the hospital.

I must close for now.

Forever yours,
David

France
January 30 1945

My Darling,

Just a few lines to let you know I'm getting along all right and feeling better than I did yesterday.

Say, how on earth can anyone go on a diet just to lose weight? I'm on a liquid diet, and I don't like it! Looks like you're going to let yourself in for a lot of cooking when I get back.

Enclosed is a Normandy patch that I got in Carentan, France. I have been reading *I Never Left Home* by Bob Hope. It's crazy but good. That guy must be nuts, still he does pretty good at it.

Darling, as you've probably noticed on this letter, I'm using my old address. Keep on writing. I'll get my mail someday.

Good-bye for now.

Forever yours,
David

France
February 2, 1945

My Darling,

Just a few words to let you know I'm okay. I hope this finds you and the family well.

Still haven't had any mail. Sure hope I'll be getting some soon, probably will. I was released from the hospital yesterday and am now on my way back to my unit, just how far I will get this time, I don't know.

I'm getting pretty damn fed up back here, so I hope I get out of here real soon.

Must close for now, darling. Keep on writing.

All my love,
David

France
February 8, 1945

My Darling,

Well, hon, I haven't been AWOL or anything. I've just been moving around some. I'll be able to write once again. I'm still not back with my unit.

I met Terry yesterday quite by accident. So once again, we're together for a while anyway. We took some pictures today. I told you about him once before. He is about 5'7" tall and has blond hair and blue eyes, I think. He's a well-built kid and is 18 years old. When I say he's a good kid, that's putting it mildly—he's tops. He doesn't have a girl back home.

He's from Pennsylvania. I hope your girl friend can write to him. There I go, playing cupid again. I promised him she would. Oh yes, he doesn't smoke or drink, so he's even a better fellow than I am, and how. I'm not giving myself much credit, am I? Well, so much for Terry.

Looks like my combat days are over, for a while anyway. That means no more airborne duty for now. I figure that within a few months, I'll give it another try. But until then, I'm not sure what my duties will be. I'm waiting to be reclassified now. Perhaps this will sound good to you, darling. But to me, it means leaving what's left of the old gang and starting in all over again. Oh well, that's life, I guess.

Terry and I went to see a GI show last night. It sure was good. They had a good band, and one fellow was a good singer. He sang "I'll Walk Alone, Always" and several other good numbers. It's the first show of its kind that I've seen for quite some time. Perhaps that's why I thought it was so good. Anyway, it was an enjoyable evening.

I must close for now, darling. Write often and keep on writing to my old unit until I'm settled down again.

All my love,
David

France
February 11, 1945

My Darling,

Just a few lines today. It's Sunday and very rainy, so it's inside for me. I'm in the dayroom close to the radio. We have no fire, and it's rather cold down here.

Terry is trying his hand at ping-pong. He just beat the devil out of me. I had some good luck a few days ago, darling. I happened to run into a kid I used to go to school with. He's been in Africa and on through. He sure has changed, but not as much as I have, I guessed, because he couldn't remember me.

I hope everyone doesn't forget what I look like. I sort of had the idea that once anyone had seen me, they couldn't forget. I guess I'm not so bad as all that though.

It looks like I'm going back to my outfit after all. I have better hopes now than I did anyway. I still won't be able to jump for a while.

They're playing "It Had to Be You." I like that very much. Must close for now, darling. Write often.

All my love,
David

France
February 18, 1945

My Darling,

Here it is Sunday again. The days are really rolling along, but not fast enough.

Terry left this morning. I sure hated to see us two guys broken up. But that's the way it goes. The buddy system just doesn't work over here. He went back to the outfit, and I don't know where I'll end up. It's hard to tell just what they'll do with me. I won't go back to the front. That's been made pretty plain to me.

It's pretty nice out today. The sun is out, and it's quite warm, still pretty much like spring. Although there will be more cold weather, I guess. Sorry there was no Valentine for you this year, darling. I didn't forget. There just weren't any to be had.

There's a church program on the radio, and it's very good. I didn't go this morning. I should have. I know that it's not every Sunday you have a chance to go.

Must close for now. I'll probably write again today, anyway. Write often.

All my love,
David

France
February 20, 1945

My Darling,

I have just returned from the movie *Destination Tokyo*. A couple of pals of mine and I went to see it even though we saw it back in the States quite some time ago.

The news is very good tonight on all fronts. It's good to know the Pacific battle is going full blast. The victories aren't easily won. We know that from experience. I have a very good friend in the paratroop unit that jumped on Corregidor. I came very close to going to the South Pacific with him. I believe I'd rather be over here.

I went to a New York State meeting last night with a friend who is from the state. I think about every nationality was present. I had a good time. They played and sang songs in Italian, Polish, and several others. I liked the Polish songs the best. You should have heard those guys argue, all in fun of course. The ones from Brooklyn even had a little disagreement over baseball. That's only natural, for that's one game they love.

I never smoked a pipe while I was at home, did I? I guess that's something else you'll have to get used to. Anyway it kind of cuts down on my ration and Terry[26] (quote) says I look very well smoking one. Of course, he really puts on. By the way, has your friend received his letter? I know he wrote to her—just what, I don't know. I could have read it, but it wasn't any of my business. I gave him her picture and told him she was a swell girl.

I must close for now, darling. Write often.

All my love,
David

---

[26] Terry and Dad became lifetime friends. Terry, whose real name is Charles Eckman, visited our family often. He called Dad the Golden Warrior.

France
March 8, 1945

My Darling,

Here's that guy again. It's rather late. But I will write as I didn't last night. It'll probably be short, but better than none.

I've really got my nose in the radio tonight, and the news is really good. They just gave out the news of the Rhine crossing. I've been sweating that out.

I've been pretty busy tonight, pressing my clothes and shining my buttons and boots. It really takes a lot of time when you do it right. I received the hometown paper today. It seems like each and every one of them have deaths and missing in action of my friends back home. But again, that's war. We have our record set fixed now and have several swell records. So we're doing a little bit of all right.

Do you hear from my folks very often? They think you're swell. I wish you could have met my father, darling. You would have liked him. He was a wonderful father. I realize it more every day.

The kids are doing swell in school. Billy is doing the best, I guess. He's a smart boy, and I encourage him all I can. He's going to be a good-looking fellow too.

Well, sweetheart, it's after ten, so good night and God bless you.

Hugs and kisses and stuff.

All my love,
David

France
March 9, 1945

Hello Mother,

Guess it's about time I write you again. I've received several letters from you in the last few days. Thanks a lot. It seems if I don't hear from Lou, I get a letter from you. That's good though; it kind of fills in the spaces.

The news is good tonight. We seem to be doing good all over the globe. I listen to the news every chance I get. Sure hope I don't have to go back again. But one never knows.

There's some beautiful music on the air tonight. How I would love to be home, just Lou and me somewhere alone. Well, I can dream, can't I? I've been doing a pretty good job of it for a long time now. One of these days, those dreams will come true.

I saw Mickey Rooney and his jeep show a couple of days ago. I forgot to tell Lou in my letter last night. He was pretty good. There were two other men with him. It was thirty minutes of good fun. He's the only star I've seen over here that I remember of. Well, I must close or now. Write when you can. Say hello to the rest of the family, and give my love to Lou.

Dave

France
March 15, 1945

Darling,

Just a few words tonight. It's been several days since I've written to you, also since I've heard from you. Sometimes, it's hard to write when you don't receive letters. But I do my best. The music is swell tonight. But what good is it to listen and dream?

We've been awarded another Presidential Citation,[27] which means we can wear a cluster in our ribbon. Enclosed is a clipping about our citation and the review we had for General Eisenhower. It's a pretty good write-up. Well so much for that.

I volunteered for a jump the other morning. But no go. They wouldn't let me do it. They're right. I know I shouldn't even think of it. But a fellow gets so darn disgusted. He'll do anything. I did want to make it as it would have been something new for me. I mean the type of jump.

I was glad to hear that you received the clippings; as for me telling you about it someday will be enough. I believe the clippings speak for themselves. I have nothing to add. I just want to make a scrapbook with them someday. I will close for now.

Love,
David

---

[27] The Presidential Unit Citation is a senior unit award granted to military units that have performed an extremely meritorious or heroic act, usually in the face of an armed enemy. Presidential Unit Citation—Wikipedia, the free encyclopedia.

France
March 19, 1945

Hello Mother,

I'm sitting outside of my tent while writing this. It's very nice out today. The sun is shining very bright, and it's really warm when you get where the wind can't hit you.

I received an eight-page letter from you today. That's the biggest letter I've had for months. But I like them when they're from you. They're very newsy, and you tell me so many things about Lou that I love to hear and she never speaks of.

No, Mother, I'll never forget the first time I came to your home. At heart, I'm still that little boy that you spoke of, much wiser in the ways of the world. Though I guess that is as it should be. You spoke of bacon and eggs, hot biscuits, and butter. That's going to be my first request the first morning I get up once I get back and cooked by you. How about that?

I went over to see Terry yesterday. I wish you could see him. He's sure a swell kid. Lots of the guys think he's my brother. He does have blue eyes and blond hair. But he's a little rascal and doesn't even come to my shoulder. He kids me about Lou all the time. We get along swell. Well, it's dinnertime. So I'll close for now.

Dave

France
March 25, 1945

My Darling,

I haven't written to you all week, so I guess I'd better get on the beam and do something about it.

I've received about five letters from you and one from Mother. So you're doing fine from your end of the line.

The news is sure great today. It seems we're well across the Rhine for good. I'm glad of that. But the war isn't over for a long time yet—if only everyone would think of it that way. I think it will last for several months yet.

I received my citation for the Bronze Star Medal[28] but not the medal itself as yet. As long as I know it's coming, that's the main thing. I'm sending the citation along. Would you mind sending it to my folks? They'll want to read it as they know nothing about my receiving it.

Well, it's raining now. I've been expecting it all day. I like to see pretty weather because of the boys on the front. It's miserable enough as it is without the rain.

Well, I'll be home in a year or so, I hope.

I must close for now. Write often as possible.

All my love,
David

---

[28] A Bronze Star Medal is for individual military decoration and the fourth highest award for bravery, heroism, or meritorious service. Bronze Star Medal (Model #124 ARBS)—USA Military Medals.

Location Unknown
April 12, 1945

I have just returned from the show *My Reputation*. It was pretty good. I've seen better though.

I received two swell letters from you, and neither of them over ten days old. So that's good.

I'm so darn disgusted and browned off tonight. Some things just don't suit me worth a damn, the drafting of nurses. If some of these so-called men had to lie in a damn hospital for a few weeks and see how little some of them have to do, not that there isn't something to do. Yes, but they let the ward boys do it. Sure, darling, there are some who are really swell and are really doing their job. But I've been in about eleven hospitals, and I think I know the score. I'd say about half of them talk about Joe or the nice handsome major they have a date with, or do it yourself.

Many nights I asked for sleeping pills or something to put me to sleep because I was in pain. Sure they said, "We'll bring it to you." Did I get it? Sometimes yes and sometimes no. But usually, I just stayed awake most of the night. Oh, I could say a lot of things. But what's the use? Anyway, I can't blow my top on paper. But when I get home, oh boy, I'll tell the good and the bad.

Now do you understand why I don't want you to join the nurses' cadets? If there was an urgent need for them, then I would say, swell. But I know better.

Must close now, darling. It's often after one, and this guy is sleepy.

All my love and kisses.

Forever yours,
David

Location Unknown
April 15, 1945

My Darling,

I received three letters from you today, January 17, 18, and 19-pretty old. But I was happy to get them. They're really marked up. But then they've been around trying to catch up with me. I'm a hard guy to catch up with.

Darling, you spoke of the Germans having the run of things at home. If only I could begin to tell you how good the Germans are treated over here. It's pitiful. It's worse in the hospitals. They treat them like kings. I can't tell you these things like I want to. I'm not that free. But when I come home, I can tell you.

You probably won't believe some of the things. I'm not asking you to. I only know what I've seen and what I see every day. I'm damn fed up with it. So are a lot of the other guys.

I'm fed up with people patting the enemy on the back. That's just what they're doing when they feel sorry for them. Oh well, those people will learn the hard way.

No, darling, it wouldn't do if you were over here with me. I often hear that discussion around here, and 99 percent say they wouldn't want their wives over here.

Must close for now, hon.

Write often. Love and kisses.

Always yours,
David

Location Unknown
April 26, 1945

My Darling,

Well, hon, I finally received a pass to Paris. I had a wonderful time. I really enjoyed myself and had a wonderful place to stay at the Grand Hotel. They really treat a fellow swell.

If I wrote about everything I saw and did, I'd probably be writing for weeks. I'd heard so much about Paris in the springtime. While I was there, the weather was beautiful and so was Paris. I went on two different tours. So I really saw about every place of interest, like the Triumph Arch, Eiffel Tower, Notre Dame, and dozens of places.

Our guide was very good and spoke perfect English, not only telling us the history of Paris, but also about the German occupation of Paris. I assure you that some of it wasn't very good to listen to. I'll tell you about it someday. I finally sent you some perfume from Paris and hope you like it.

I went to a dance one night and a nightclub on another night. Both were really beautiful places. It's the first nightclub I'd been in since leaving the states. I'd almost forgotten what it was like. I thought it cost a lot back home. But boy, those places are cheap. I mean these places here really put it to you.

Well, darling, this is it for now. Please write a little more often.

All my love,
David

Location Unknown
May 10, 1945

My Darling,

Sure hope this letter finds you well, Lou. I'm getting along okay.

Well, darling, this part of the war is over that we've all been looking forward to. But what now? That is what about three million men are asking themselves, and I'm no exception. I've got all sorts of ideas and none of them add up to anything.

Somehow, I don't believe I'll be home for a long time yet though. It's really hard to say. I'd love to come home this summer. We could be married, and who knows? I know our time would be short. But if I could only have those parts come true. That's all I would ask before going on to the other front.

This is about all the time I have, sweetheart. Please write. Two letters in three weeks isn't much you know.

All my love and kisses,
David

Austria
May 18, 1945

My Dearest Darling,

Well, I'm through traveling for a while, I think. I hope. I've seen a lot of country though, so I'm not kicking about it.

I really don't think I should write to you. But I'm a softhearted son of a gun. Darling, I haven't been hearing from you at all, two little letters in three weeks. Oh, I know you'll probably say I haven't been writing either. Of course not, as I haven't been in one place long enough. I've been all over France, Germany, and now, Austria.

I had hoped that I would at least have one letter from you when I arrived here, but not one. I had mail, but I felt like tearing it up because all I wanted was a letter from you. Oh well, maybe I'll hear tomorrow. I doubt it. This is the first time it's ever been like this. Guess I'm away from home a little too long.

Well, kid, I don't have enough points to get out of the army, so that's that. They say I'm in A-1 condition, which is wrong. My leg bothers me all the time. Every time I hear an explosion, I go off my nut and want to hide in a hole. Oh hell, what am I telling you for? I think it will be at least a year, if not longer, before I come back. That's a long time, isn't it?

I'm now in Kosson, Austria, near Berchtesgaden, where Hitler had his famous hideout, the Eagles Nest.[29] It's really beautiful country. I'm really up in the mountains, but it's nice. I'm living

---

[29] The so-called Eagle's Nest was built as a teahouse for Adolf Hitler's fiftieth birthday. Perched on a mountain summit, its unusual position makes of the daring project a unique engineering feat. History of Hitler's Eagle's Nest, the Kehlsteinhaus.

in a hotel, swimming, riding, and fishing, etc. Of course, I work a little and operate a radio about eight hours a day

Well, darling, this has been quick, and it's rather short. But you've been on my mind so much I just had to write. I'll write again as soon as I hear from you. Give my regards to the family.

All my love,
David

CHAPTER IX

WOUNDED IN HOLLAND

God and a soldier all people adore In time of war, but not before; And when war is over and all things are righted, God is neglected and an old soldier slighted.

—Anonymous

Austria
May 27, 1945

My Darling,

It's really been beautiful here today. I've been swimming all afternoon. I've found a small cove down the river with a little sandy beach, and as far as I know, I'm the only one who knows of it so far. It's so quiet and peaceful, not a soul to disturb you.

When I returned about 4:30, I found five letters from you and one from your mother waiting for me. So I've had a perfect day. So you like shrimp? I didn't know that, darling. So do I. So you'd better learn to prepare it. I haven't had any since I've been overseas.

I'd sure love to see the movie *A Tree Grows in Brooklyn*. I have read the book. However, I doubt if the picture is anything like it. That's the way it usually is.

Fitz is here in my room, reading his darn old Boston paper—not only that, but teasing the life out of me. He's a good guy though. We're listening to the Jack Benny program. He's a scream tonight, as usual. I've always liked his program.

I don't think I told you about the radio I have now. It's a German army receiving set. Of course, I had to hook up a speaker and a few other things, for it. But it works very good. I even have a set of headphones so I can lie in bed and play it and not disturb my buddy. Pretty good, huh? I'm not lazy. I just believe in comfort.

So you had a date with a sailor? Somehow I wish you hadn't told me. Oh, I can't blame you. After all, there's probably not one girl in a thousand who has remained as true to their man as you have to me. So I won't say anymore.

Darling, unless they lower the point number, I'm just stuck. I only have eighty. Count it yourself: Purple Heart, bronze star, and four battle stars plus service. I think the single men got a rotten deal on the points for fathers.

I've been through all that some of my buddies have. Yet some of them have children and those points were enough to carry them over. Oh well, that's army for you. I'll at least get a furlough if I should go to the Pacific. Right now, just don't worry about me. I'm safe and having a good rest. What more could I ask for other than being with you? Oh yes, I haven't gotten a cluster for my Purple Heart yet from Bastogne. If—and when—I do, that will give me the 85 points. However, somebody messed up the records, and I probably won't get it. It's really my fault. At the time, I wasn't interested in any darn old cluster for anything. I just wanted to get away from there or go nuts.

Now that my mail isn't censored, I can tell you how and when I was wounded in Holland. I'll make it brief. I just thought you might like to know.

It was September 22, 1944, near St. Oedennrode, Holland, at a forward observation post. At the forward observation post and CP, I was very tired that morning and didn't have to go as I hadn't slept for 48 hours. However, the day before, the British had given tank support, and we also had it for that morning.

We had kicked the hell out of them the day before. The Colonel[30] asked if I was to be his radio operator that morning, and I said yes, I wanted to be in on it. He was a hell of a swell guy. Anyway,

---

[30] Dad served as a radio operator for Colonel Cole, Colonel Michaelis and Colonel Steve Chappius. His position as a radio communications man with Regimental Headquarters was very demanding especially when relaying critical orders and directives from high-ranking colonels.

the attack had just gotten under way, and there was a devil of an explosion over our heads. That's about all I remembered for 48 hours. When I came to my senses, I thought my leg was gone. That's one terrible feeling.

I think a million things must have flashed through my head at once. I probably shouldn't have told you this. But you've asked several times, and I couldn't then. The same shell killed two and wounded five. I guess it was quite a mess, not as bad as some I've seen though. Well, enough about that.

Look, sweetheart, I've gone beyond my limit now. Oh, I could ramble on, but I've got some work to do.

Always yours,
David

Austria
May 27, 1945

Dear Mother,

I'd begun to think you were angry with me for writing that letter to Lou.

Thank God you aren't—anything but that. I didn't mean for it to hurt you or anyone for that matter. I should have never written it in the first place. But I hadn't heard from anyone in a while. I'm sorry if I hurt your feelings.

I know Lou is true to me, and I do trust her. She could have a thousand dates and not be untrue to me, and I still wouldn't lose my faith in her. That's something I really cling to since I've been over here. I'm just tired and fed up with the hell of war and smell of death.

You needn't worry about me volunteering for the SP. I'm just full of patriotism. Ha. Yes, my knees are shaking. No, I have had my fill. I've volunteered for too many things already, and what has that gotten me? From now on, I follow orders.

Well, Mother, I guess I'd better close shop for tonight. Write as often as you can. Give my regards to everyone.

Your son (to be),
David

Austria
May 30, 1945

My Darling,

I just returned from the show *Francisco Sal*, or something like that. My memory must be getting very bad. It was pretty good anyway.

I'm really hitting the dirt, darling, using scrap paper and enemy envelopes. Don't suppose you mind though as long as you hear from me. We had a memorial service today for our fallen comrades. It was pretty sad as the names were read off the list. Guys you used to kid around with, your old buddies. They're really the ones that made the victory in Europe possible. I hope that everyone will always remember that. They gave their lives that we might carry on. We have done that. We must not fail them now.

Darling, I'm glad you want to see *Objective Burma*. I saw it a few nights ago. I hope it gives you a brief idea of what our job is. It wasn't quite as real as it could have been. But there's a limit on pictures sometimes. I wish there wasn't. The people at home really don't know what the boys go through though; they think they know. But nothing is like the real thing. Let's talk about something more pleasant.

I'm going fishing tomorrow, sweetheart. Want to come along? It's about an hour and a half hike. I have the whole day off though. I know where there is a beautiful small lake, and as far as I know, no one except me knows of it—soldiers I mean. We could have a wonderful time. Only I probably wouldn't catch any fish. I wouldn't even try.

Well, sugar, I'd better sign off and get some sleep. I'll need it. Write often.

All my love always,
David

Austria
May 31, 1945

My Darling,

It's been a very dreary day, rainy and foggy. I didn't get to go fishing. Instead, I've spent the day inside, working on my radio equipment and making leather for my knife.

It's a Hitler youth knife and has "Blut and Ehre" written on the blade. That means "blood and iron." I think this was the Bismark's motto.

It's swell to be inside on a day like this. I'd hate to be in a foxhole today. It would be miserable. I even hate to think about it.

How about some more ideas on our postwar plans, darling? I think going to Alaska is out. So let's forget about that. Five children? Well, I think that is two too many. I think so now, anyway. God knows what you can convince me of. One thing for sure, darling, I'll never be happy with an inside job.

Did you ever hear of an old saying "Never take a city girl to the country?" Tell me, Lou, have you any idea of the work a farmer's wife does? I wonder if you really do. There's a million chores to do morning and night, milking, feeding, taking care of the chickens, and housework. Of course, the man takes care of the outside work as much as possible, but in the spring, summer, and fall, when one is putting his crops in and harvesting in the fall, he works early and late. So the work near the house falls on his wife. Perhaps I'm painting a rather bad picture of it for you. But it is a lot of hard work for a couple just starting out. I'm just saying it's going to be my job after the war. But the idea of a farm can have a little place in my mind.

I'm starting a class in forestry. Though there are only three of us, the Captain has decided to have a class anyway. We will have our own instructor and a man from this area who knows how to climb and has been in the forest service all of his life. It's a chance to learn something, and we receive credit for it.

Must close for now. Please write often. All my love.

Always yours,
David

Austria
June 6, 1945

My Darling,

It is D-365, and I'm still kicking. One year ago today, I was a very scared lad. First I was mad, then I was scared, and then both of them. That was one day I shall never forget. I pray that in my future years, I shall never live such a year as this past one has been.

The pictures I had taken at Berchtesgaden are ready, hon. Everyone tells me I look very sad and old. In fact, they asked me if I was ready to cry. So you probably won't like them at all. I'll send them out today.

I'm not giving you any hope. But rumors are that I'll be coming home around August or September. Don't pin your hopes on it. That's strictly talk.

You go right ahead and buy those pajamas, hon. I'll try and remember what they're used for. Ha. Look, darling, there's no sense in buying anything valuable for my birthday. But use your own judgment.

Oh yes, I've been wanting to ask you something. Do you think you'll still want a short engagement? I might consider 4 or 5 days. I am thinking what kind of a husband I will make a woman as sweet as you are. I have no skill for a good job. I haven't the education a man should have. Why, there's lots of things I can think of. But I'm not worried about it. As long as we love each other, then we'll do all right.

Must close for now. Write often. Give my regards to the family.

All my love and kisses,
David

Mittersill, Austria
June 10, 1945

My Darling,

I've just returned from a tiresome trip and was I ever happy to
find eight letters waiting for me, all from the Livingstone family,
with five of them from you.

Gee, but I was happy because I haven't had much mail for several
days. It's been pretty cold here today. The clouds are hanging all
over the mountainsides. The roads are slick, making driving a
little dangerous. So we had to travel pretty slow.

Darling, I'm sorry about my letter about the sailor. I had no right
to write that, but I just couldn't help it. I hadn't heard from you
for a while, and well, a fellow can think a million things. Please
kick me in the pants for me when I come home for it. I do trust
you to the utmost, darling. Please believe me.

Personally, I don't think I'll be over here for more than a few more
months, that is my opinion. But if I should be, hon, it's for the
best. Please remember that because if I come home soon then I'll
go on to the South Pacific. However, I assure you I'd be willing
to do that just to be with you for a few weeks. I know that you
understand it takes a good trouper to see things through.

Darling, you say there are many times when you feel like writing
and telling me of your troubles, then please do. What am I for?
I might as well get used to them, and besides, I want to hear and
know about them. So don't keep anything from me.

Yes, I still have the little bundle of joy with me. He's in good
shape to. His picture is a little creased and worn but all together. I
can't begin to tell you how many times a week I take him out and
look at him. Why, he's no trouble at all. Yes, he is a symbol of the

future, and the first one had better be a boy. I'd be just as happy with a little girl though. Wouldn't you?

Enclosed is a little something I hope you will like, darling. I bought two of them and will send this one and keep the other one in case this doesn't get to you. Wear it, hon, that's what it's for.

I must close for now. Write often. Good night, sweetheart.

All my love and kisses,
David

PS: I put personal on this because you might not want your mother to read it to you. It doesn't really matter to me. She probably knows more about us that we think anyway. Most mothers do.

CHAPTER X

BATTLES, CAMPAIGNS AND PHOTOGRAPHS

*The difference between one man and another
is not mere ability—it is energy.*

—Thomas Arnold, English educator

David Clinton Tharp

June 16, 1924-January 24, 1999

Bushnell Veteran Cemetery
Buried with full military honors

Battles and Campaigns: Ardennes, Normandy, Rhineland, and Central Europe

Presidential Unit Citation (2) awarded to the 101st Airborne Division for Normandy and the Battle of Bastogne. See General Dwight D. Eisenhower's March 15, 1945 speech on opposite page.

The Presidential Unit Citation is the second highest award a unit can receive.

Purple Heart with Oak Leaf Cluster for battle wounds in Holland, September 1944 and Battle of the Bulge, January 4, 1945.

Combat Infantryman's Badge

Bronze Star with Oak Leaf Cluster and "V" Device for Valor.

* In US Military, Oak Leaf Clusters on ANY medal indicate multiple awards of that medal.

EAME Theater Ribbon w/4 Ribbon w/4 Bronzes w/bronze Arrowhead.

Orange Lanyard Awarded by Holland, The Netherlands.

Honorable Discharge, November 20, 1945.

PRESIDENTIAL CITATION

Following is the speech given by the Supreme Commander, Gen. Dwight D. Eisenhower on March 15, 1945 at Mourmelon-le-Grand, France in presenting the 101st Airborne Division "The Presidential Citation" for their heroic action in Bastogne during the "Battle of the Bulge".

The Presentation

"It is a great personal honor for me to be here today to take part in a ceremony that is unique in American history. Never before has a full division been cited by the War Department, in the name of the President, for gallantry in action. This day marks the beginning of a new tradition in the American army. With that tradition, therefore, will always be associated the name of the 101st Airborne Division and of Bastogne."

"Yet you men, because you are soldiers of proved valor and of experience, would be the last to claim that you are the bravest and the best. All the way from where the Marines are fighting on Iwo Jima through the Philippines and Southeast Asia, on through the Mediterranean, and along the great front and on the Russian frontiers, are going forward, day by day, those battles sustained by the valor of you and other Allied units, that are beating this enemy to his knees. They are proving for once and for all that dictatorship cannot produce better soldiers than can an aroused democracy."

"In many of these actions are units that have performed with unexcelled brilliance. So far as I know there may be many among you that would not rate Bastogne as your bitterest battle. Yet, it is entirely fitting and appropriate that you should be cited for that particular battle. It happened to be one of those occasions when the position itself was of utmost importance to the Allied forces. You in reserve were hurried forward and told to hold that position. All the elements of drama, of battle drama, were there. You were cut off; you were surrounded. Only valor, complete self confidence in yourselves and in you leaders, a knowledge that you were well trained, only the determination to win, could sustain soldiers under these conditions. You were given a marvelous opportunity, and you met every test."

"Therefore, you become a fitting symbol on which the United Nations, all the citizens of the United Nations, can say to their soldiers today, "We are proud of you," as it is my great privilege to say to you today, the 101st Division and all its' attached units, "I am awfully proud of you."

"With this great honor goes also a certain responsibility. Just as you are the beginning of a new tradition, you must realize each of you that from now on, the spotlight will beat on you with particular brilliance. Whenever you say you are a soldier of the 101st Division, everybody, whether it's on the street in the city or on the front line, will expect unusual conduct from you. I know that you will meet every test of the future like you did in Bastogne."

"Good luck and God be with each one of you."

~ General Dwight D. Eisenhower

Dad before battle

Dad after battle

Dad with his helmet on and his 101st Airborne comrades

Dad in Paris

Le Palais de Chaillot   Paris, France

CITATION FOR THE BRONZE STAR MEDAL

Private First Class David-C. Tharp, 16 335 101, Parachute Infantry, while serving with the Army of the United States, distinguished himself by meritorious service in action. During the period 6 June to 28 December 1944 he performed the duties of a radio operator in a superior manner. During the Normandy campaign, he operated his radio at forward observation posts and directed devastating artillery fire on the enemy. He also accompanied numerous reconnaissance and combat patrols affording excellent radio communication at all times. In the Holland campaign, he performed his duties under hazardous enemy artillery fire but afforded to the regimental commander excellent radio service until he became wounded by enemy fire. During the siege of Bastogne, Belgium, despite the fact that enemy artillery fire had scored direct hits on the building in which he was operating his radio, he remained at his post and operated his radio in an efficient and skillful manner. His actions were in accordance with the highest standards of the military service. Entered military service from Indiana.

Citation For The Bronze Star Medal

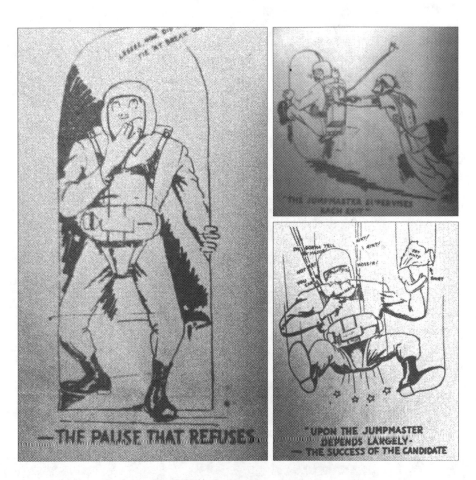

Army Parachute Jumping Cartoons

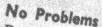

Article About Concern Over Soldier's Return Home
We need to understand what goes on in the mind and heart of a soldier during war. War wreaks havoc on the human soul. Dad needed the letters as an escape from what was going on around him & the changes occurring within. He was & continued to suffer after the war from PTSD, something we knew very little about during WWII.

Sweetheart Paratrooper Envelope Referenced
in January 15, 1943 letter

Paratrooper Post Card

Paratrooper Christmas Card December 1943

Dad & Charles Eckman (Terry)
in Europe-They became life long friends

David & Betty Lou, his sweetheart

Betty Lou & David

David & Betty's Wedding Day in March, 1946

Dachau book cover published by Army in 1945 after liberating the concentration camp

FOREWORD

DACHAU, 1933 - 1945, will stand for all time as one of history's most gruesome symbols of inhumanity. There our troops found sights, sounds and stenches horrible beyond belief, cruelties so enormous as to be incomprehensible to the normal mind. DACHAU and death were synonymous.

No words or pictures can carry the full impact of these unbelievable scenes but this report presents some of the outstanding facts and photographs in order to emphasize the type of crime which elements of the SS committed thousands of times a day, to remind us of the ghastly capabilities of certain classes of men, to strengthen our determination that they and their works shall vanish from the earth.

The sections comprising this report were prepared by the agencies indicated. They remain substantially as they were originally submitted in the belief that to consolidate this material in a single literary style would seriously weaken its realism.

WILLIAM W. QUINN
Colonel, G.S.C.
A.C. of S.G.2
7th U.S. Army

This Book Entitled Dachau was published by the Army in 1945 after liberating the concentration camp. It contains horrific photos of the genocide and was brought home by our father to prove that it did take place. The book was later donated by our mother, Betty Lou and now sits on display at the Maitland Memorial Holocaust Museum in Maitland, Florida along with her beautiful sculpture of a concentration camp survivor called, "I Accuse."

Mom & Dad at one of many 101st Airborne Annual Reunions

101st Airborne Reunion-Dad is top center. We
attended many of these annual reunions over the years
as a family and met the German interrogator and
interpreter that worked with the Americans.

David C. Tharp,Regimental
HQ 502 PIR.Radioman van
kolonel Michaelis.

Bob Salley,Gene Kobey,? en
Bob Likam.Allen van het
326e Engineer Batalion.

November 1985.Reunie in
Chicago.

101st Airborne Reunion in Chicago, Illinois in 1985. Peter
Hendrikx of Holland is shown with Dad upper left inset.
Peter travelled extensively over the years attending many
reunions and interviewing the 101st Airborne. In 2012, Peter
published the book, "Orange is the Color of The Day" with
an extensive pictorial of the 101st Airborne. Peter Hendrick's
website which honors American soldiers who are laid to rest in
his country at the U.S. Military Cemetery in Margraten, the
Netherlands can be visited at www.heroesatmargraten.com

Dad with youngest son, David and grandson, David, Jr.

The Daily Commercial article on Dad June 5, 1994. Dad
displays his medals. The 101st Airborne Division was dropped
and parachuted behind Utah Beach on June 5, 1944 around
midnight. The paratroopers mission was dangerous because
they were dropped in enemy territory in the middle of the
night. "It was kind of scary. You knew that some of you
weren't going to come back," said David Tharp in The Daily
Commercial interview for the 50th D-Day anniversary in 1994

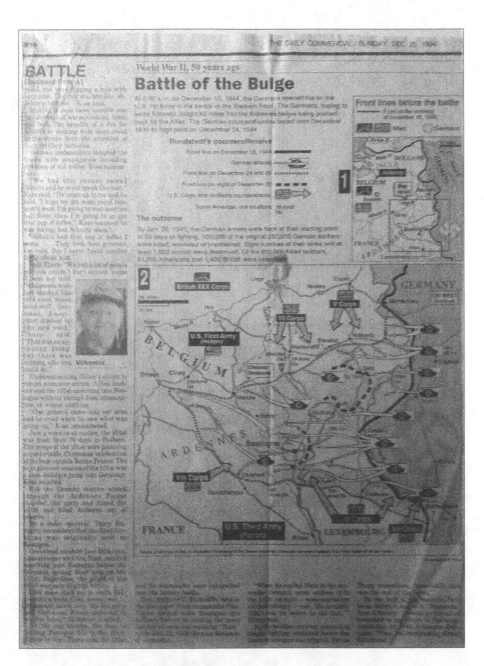

The Daily Commercial interview from 12/25/94

Tharp Sees
Youth Gains
Tie to Port

Dad in contemplation while walking along the Indiana Dunes shoreline. While in office as Portage Chamber of Commerce President, he addressed the association by saying, "I was happy to shake the sand of the Normandy beaches out of my boots 20 years ago, and I'll be happier still to shake the sand of a barren stretch of land out of my shoes to give Indiana her gateway to the world."

Dad wearing his Screaming Eagle hat.

Castle Rolle in Champs Belgium where the
101st Airborne set up headquarters

Our oldest brother David met with Madame Rolle in 2004 during
a trip to Europe and was surprised to find not only Castle Rolle but
Madame Rolle who was just a young girl when the 101st Airborne
was there at her parents home. She remembered our Dad as a "nice
young fellow who kept talking to someone named Roger . . ." As
a radio operator, Dad would keep saying "Roger in, Roger out."

David Clinton Tharp's photo hangs among the gallery of Izaak
Walton League Presidents of the Miller Chapter in Indiana

Dad 1943

Dad with his dog, 1943

Lt. Col. Robert G. Cole
CO 3rd Bn., 502nd PIR

Col. John H. Michaelis
CO 502nd PIR

Lt. Col. Steve A. Chappui
CO 2nd Bn., 502nd PIR

These are the Colonels that Dad worked with when
communicating vital radio transmissions.
Photograph source: Orange is the Color of the Day

Parachute training

Dad 1944

Tom Pastorius, friend and comrade 502ⁿᵈ PIR

Russell Miller, comrade 502nd PIR receiving an award

101ˢᵗ Airborne 502ⁿᵈ PIR comrades

Dad in Mittersill, Austria 1945

Richard Ladd 101st Airborne, 502nd PIR shown here in both photos with fellow comrade and the infamous 502nd regimental insignia with bat wings, skull and parachute. We had the good fortune of meeting Richard and his lovely wife, Helen He remembered seeing Dad the day before they jumped into Holland and many years later at a 101st reunion in 1994. They recognized each other instantly. Richard called the radio men "communicators"

Robert J. Harle 101st Airborne, 502nd PIR. I had the pleasure of
meeting Mr. Harle in 2013 who fondly remembered Dad as a
soft-spoken man. Mr. Harle was also a radio communicator who
received the Bronze Star Medal. Dad and Bob Harle shared English
barracks while they prepared for their first jump into Normandy.

Dad's father, my grandfather, Ibren

Dad's mother, Jennie Tharp, my grandmother and namesake

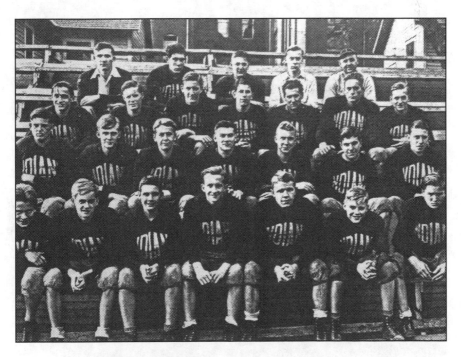

Dad is pictured here second row from top, second one inset. He played high school football with Gil Hodges in Petersburg, Indiana 1939-1940

Dad top center with his brothers and sisters in 1948

Mom & Dad in 1996

CHAPTER XI

DISPLACED PERSONS

Most people coming out of war feel lost and resentful. What had been a minute-to-minute confrontation with yourself, your struggle with what courage you have against discomfort, at the least, and death at the other end, ties you to the people you have known in the war and makes for a time others seem alien and frivolous.

—Lillian Hellman, American playwright

Mittersill, Austria
June 11, 1945

My Darling,

This is my day off, and I'm staying in as I'm not feeling so good, just a headache.

I'm listening to an English program. Honest, darling, they're as corny as, well, I don't know. Their jokes are as old as the hills. Tell me, do you see any English pictures back there?

I have a furlough coming up one of these days, either to France or England. It will probably be a couple of months, if I'm still around. Well, they're getting the educational program rolling now. I'm starting a class in German tomorrow. I plan to enroll. I speak it a little, but I can learn a lot from the class I know.

I'm in the forestry class but may drop this later though as another fellow and myself want to go to a school, and it's quite a ways from here. We're working on that now. If I get to go, it will mean that I'll be here for at least one year. I don't like that, but it's worthwhile, darling. When I come back to you, I want to stay not just for a few days and take off again. I think you'll agree to that. Well, it's time that I go to work, so I'll close for now. Write often.

All my love and kisses,
David

Mittersill, Austria
June 14, 1945

Hello My Darling,

Would you like to hear from a very disgusted and browned-off soldier?

All kidding aside, it's past eleven, and somehow, I just had to write to you tonight. We were just told tonight what would happen to us in the future. Men with over 85 points will go home and be discharged. Men with less (that's me) will go to the Pacific in the future. They didn't say whether we would get furloughs in the States or not. But I'm sure we will because some of us have a year and a half to two years over here, with plenty of combat time to our credit.

If they don't give us a leave first, the morale is going to be mighty damn low. I don't think there is one of us who are not willing to go to the Pacific if they'll give us a leave home first. Don't worry about it though. They can't keep us apart forever, that's for sure.

While looking around today, I happened to find some pictures of the last war. I'm trying to decide whether I should keep them or not. They're quite interesting—the uniforms they wore, the type of equipment they used. Some of it will make you laugh when you think of what we have today.

All my love,
David

Mittersill, Austria
June 16, 1945

My Darling,

This has been a beautiful day though it's raining right now.

Well, this marks my twenty-first birthday. I wonder where I will be on my next one. I received a registered letter from the family in England wishing me all the best, as they say. They were pretty swell to me.

I went to Berchtesgaden last night and was it ever cold coming back. I installed my radio in the jeep, so we had music going up and coming back.

I received my Bronze Star Medal yesterday at a ceremony. It's not a very beautiful medal. But the ribbon is rather pretty though. My Purple Heart Cluster came through too. But by a miscount, I still have only eighty points, kind of tough, but that's the way it stands.

Well, I must get up early in the morning. So for now, it's good night.

All my love,
David

Mittersill, Austria
June 20, 1945

My Darling,

I'm the happiest tonight, really up in the clouds. The reason is that I received three wonderful letters from you and one from your mother.

One of your letters was written on D-day or, rather, a year later, I should say. You'll never know all the things that ran in and out of my mind during that plane ride across the channel, darling. It took my plane about two and a half hours, as I remember now. I had plenty of time to think about you. You may not believe it. But I actually went to sleep for a few minutes and somebody yelled, "There's the coast of France below now." Well, I was wide-awake then and how.

I never told you before but I was in the first wave of troops into France that night. I jumped number right man in the stick. That may sound terrible to you, I mean being in the first plane and all. But actually, it was good because the Germans didn't have time to get their ack-ack[31] range targeting the first plane. The ones that came in later caught hell though. In Holland, I was in the first plane in the second wave.[32] My plane caught hell there. But the pilot held his course, and we got out all right. Those air corps boys are swell guys, and I'll always say well done to each and every one of them. Say, I didn't mean to get off on this subject.

---

[31] Ack-ack: Anti-aircraft guns usually with multi-barrels with 4 or 6 barrels

[32] Paratroopers went through some of the most vigorous and difficult training in the war and were considered among the elite soldiers in the war.

Hon, you're going to be getting some new rolls of film. They'll be something to show our children. Maybe I can even dig up a yarn or two for them also. Who knows?

That's all right about my birthday, kid. Buy a bond instead as that will suit me better. I just hope I'm home in time for your birthday in September. You'll get something extra special.

So you received a picture of Billy and Betty? That was swell of my grandma. But then she's a wonderful person. There was a time when I didn't realize it. I do now.

I've had this wallpaper in front of me all this time and have finally decided that I like it. You bet it looked kind of funny to me at first. But honest, I do like it. I'll bet the room will really look swell.

Write often and, yes, even while you're on your leave.

All my love,
David

Mittersill, Austria
June 21, 1945

My Darling,

I received two more letters from you today. You're really keeping my morale up. Believe me, I need it.

I wish I could begin to tell you how I feel about this fraternizing over here. It would take a book. I see it going on every day, and it burns me up. But what the hell can one person do about it? It's only a small fine to these guys, and they don't care. It's disgusting as hell. I've seen too many American lives lost to have anything to do with these people at all.

I can't forget all of the things of the past. When it comes to dealing with these people, I don't want to. All I can say is that the Americans are too easy on them. Well, enough of that.

There's some talk about making an album of the 101st Airborne with battle pictures and all. I hope they do. It'll really be something worthwhile.

Perhaps this fall will see me home. Well, sweetheart, I must close for now. Write often.

Always yours,
David

Mittersill, Austria
June 22, 1945

My Darling Lou,

Just don't you worry about the bacon-and-eggs breakfast for my homecoming. Perhaps we can live on love.

I don't usually tell these jokes, but this one goes like this about a young married couple. He knew she couldn't cook when he married her. Anyway, he said they could live on love. So on the first day he came home from work. There was the young bride sitting in front of the fireplace. "Where's my supper," he says. "I'm warming it," as she sat in front of the fire.

I guess I'm not very good at jokes. I don't know what ever made me think of that. Well, so much for that.

We've been reading in the paper all the time about the meat shortage back home. And from what you say, it's pretty rough. For a while, our food was terrible. It's better now though. Why we even had chicken today.

You were a little wrong about my points. Here they are:
    30 months service
    15 months overseas
    20 (four battle stars, France, Holland, and Belgium)
    10 (Purple Heart with cluster, central Germany)
    15 (Bronze Star)
    80 points total

All my love,
David

Mittersill, Austria
June 23, 1945

Hello Darling,

Well, the company had a farewell party tonight for the 85 pointers
who are leaving soon.

I didn't go. You probably wonder why. There are several reasons.
I don't drink at all anymore, and there were a lot of drunks.
For women, they had what they call DPs, displaced persons[33]:
Russians, Polish, and God knows what all. I guess it wasn't so bad
to have them there.

I did stop in for a few minutes as I helped the Captain install
the loud speaking system, and I noticed several German women
in the place. Oh, they had DP armbands on too, the two-faced
people they are. I'm sick of this occupation, Lou. If it's like this
now, then just what will it be like a few years from now?

Really, I can't begin to tell you how much I hate these people.
You can believe me or not. I have plenty of reason to believe them
and like them now. Like hell I have. So they're good German
people now? We shouldn't be so tough with them? One day we
are enemies, and the next we're friends? That's some people's
opinion. It sure as the devil isn't mine. Every damn one of them
will kill you if they get a chance. Why must the American people
be so damned stupid? I can't understand all this at all. They train
you to kill and give no ground. You've seen good American lives
lost in battle. Yet one month after the war is over, I see all of

---

[33] Displaced persons were mostly Eastern Europeans: people who
      were unable or unwilling to return to their native countries after
      WWII. Displaced Person Transportation, post-World War II.

this.[34] Perhaps I'm not very smart, but I can't understand it all. I guess I better shut up. I could write page after page on this.

I know for sure now that my future is, first, home and then the Pacific. So perhaps you won't want to marry me when I come home. Anyway, it's something to think about. I think I'll be home this fall sometime. That's just my opinion.

Must close for now. Good night and sweet dreams. Write often.

Always yours.
Love and kisses,
David

---

[34] There were signs of PTSD, post-traumatic stress disorder, during and after the war. Although there were some programs implemented, it is nothing as we know it today. Dad would suffer from terrible headaches over the years and would always moan in his sleep.

Mittersill, Austria
June 30, 1945

I received your letter today, and it was wonderful too, the kind I love to get.

You must be getting my letters pretty good now. You also said you received the pin I sent you. I'm glad you like it, darling.

Hon, you say I don't look well in some of the pictures I sent you. You must remember they were taken just after I'd gotten out of the hospital, and I wasn't well. I wasn't feeling too good either.

Don't worry about me bringing German guns home. I will probably even sell the hunting rifle I have. I've been offered a good price for it.

I received a photo today that was taken when the Colonel pinned the Star on me. I'll send it home soon. He asked me where all my ribbons were, and I told him I didn't wear them. But he said to wear them. So I will.

All my love,
David

Mittersill, Austria
July 3, 1945

My Darling,

I received a wonderful letter from you today, so I must answer tonight.

I haven't written for a couple of days. I've been very busy day and night. I had some diagrams on radio tubes, and we had to copy most of them, not hard, but very tiresome.

Enclosed are some more pictures around here and up at Berchtesgaden. It's raining like heck out and has been for two days, off and on. It even snowed last night, not down here in the valley, but up on the mountaintops. The rains had melted most of the snow, and this morning, they were white and pretty again. Guess it will go away again if this rain keeps up.

I don't think we shall ever take each other for granted, darling—at least, I hope not. I know what you mean though. I've known couples that just seemed to consider each other necessary. We must never let ourselves be that way. Oh, it's hard to tell you these things on paper.

I have the pictures of my brothers and sisters here in front of me. I can't call them kids anymore though. They've grown so much and look so healthy. I've worried about them a lot, thinking what would happen to them if I should lose my grandmother. It was Father's wish that no matter what happened, they would never be put in a home.

I must close for tonight, sweetheart. Write often, please.

All my love always,
David

Auxerre, France
July 7, 1945

Darling,

I got more mail from you again yesterday. It's really swell, and you're writing regular. That's the best way to keep my morale up until I come home.

Yes, I've gained my weight back and now weigh 186 pounds. That's not bad. At least, I'm not fat at all. As you said, who knows? I might be at home for Christmas. I think so now. But one never knows. One day you hear something good, and the next, you hear something bad. So they keep one guessing.

I want to tell you about this educational program that we have or, rather, the one you hear so much about. So far, all I've been told about is courses requiring at least two years of college. It seems that they're giving a man who already has an education a chance to better himself and to hell with the guy who doesn't have one or hasn't had a chance to complete it. I blew my top yesterday and told them about it. It doesn't do any good though.

It seems that the only thing for me is to take a correspondence course. I have already written my high school for information on how many credits I need and what subject I must take in order to get them. I want you to know that I am interested in this education, darling. My education will have a lot to do with our future.

About the GI Bill of Rights for the soldier, I don't believe in it at all. It's probably like everything else; the army has their fingers in with so much damn red tape that very few people will mess or bother with it. Anyway, I've got enough money saved that I can go to school without working, but I'd want to work along anyway.

Write often. Give my regards to the family, and remind your mother that it's been a long time since I've had a letter from her.

Always yours,
David

Mittersill, Austria
July 14, 1945

My Darling,

I just came back from the swimming pool, really refreshing after a day in the field. The water is pretty cool though.

I've been out on the rifle range today. I did pretty good—at least, I didn't miss the target, not even at 300 yards. Guess I'll be good stuff if I have to go to the Pacific.

I'm listening to the "Grand Ole Opera." I know you don't like those barn dances and the old music. So when we're married, I'll tuck an extra radio away in my workshop. Ha. Is that okay? We'll see.

As I came back from the pool, I gathered some flowers along the stream. I've enclosed a sample for you.

Well, I think I'll crawl in between those two beautiful white sheet and pass off into dreamland. Perhaps you'll be there. Write soon.

Always yours,
David

Mittersill, Austria
July 15, 1945

My Darling,

Today is one of those that makes one wish he were starting for the seashore with the little woman tucked under one arm and the steering wheel in the other.

Yes, it's one of those days that make dreaming so easy. Life seems to have meaning, and it would be possible to find a little happiness regardless of the fact the army has a heavy hand upon your shoulder. In fact, one might feel so light as to break forth with a cheer and a whistle and remember the days of freedom and independence experienced so long ago.

What I'm trying to say is that perhaps there is still a slender hope or thread on which one can climb back to a normal life free from the greedy, thoughtless, inconsiderate, and prejudiced grasp of this stinking, unforgettable, demoralizing spirit-breaking war.

I feel as if I could go on and on. But by now, you're probably wondering what has gotten in to me. My longing is to be with you and enjoy life with you and have all the things a young couple should have. For the time being, it's impossible.

But someday, our dreams and plans will come true. Until that day comes, we'll just have to make the best of life and go on dreaming.

Always yours,
David

Austria,
July 16, 1945

My Darling,

Your letter of July 10th from Washington arrived today. I'm glad you're having a nice vacation with your grandparents.

I wish I could have been there and gone swimming with you. I remember well one night when you and your sisters were swimming at the pool, and I was outside the fence looking in. Little did I realize then that I might plan to marry you someday, and while I'm on the subject, darling, you will marry me, won't you?

If you should not want to marry upon my return, then there isn't much for me to say. It takes two people to make a bargain, you know. So it falls on upon your shoulder, that is, for one exception. If, when, I come home for my leave and think that I shall go on to the Pacific, then there will be no marriage. I have my reasons for that.

If I have to go to war against Japan, then I want to go Airborne as I've been through this war over here. And the risk and danger would be a little too much. Therefore, I would rather not be married. I have a funny feeling abut the war over there if I should have to go. I'm hoping I won't go. I think I've had it and believe I'd crack up.

I hope you found my family well during your visit to Washington. I'm sure my grandmother was more than glad to show you the things I treasure. It isn't much.

I must close now, darling. Please write often.

Always yours,
David

CHAPTER XII

THE INTERVIEW

If everybody's thinking alike, somebody isn't thinking.

—General George S. Patton,
American commander, WWII

Mittersill, Austria
July 21, 1945

My Dearest,

It is so hard for me to write. I cannot express myself as I wish. I believe you understand what I am trying to say.

The longer I stay here, the more I want to get away—anywhere would do as long as there were no Germans around. I suppose I'm just not the type for this occupation. How can the big shots say we have torn down what it took the Nazi years to build up? These people will be good to us as long as we are here. They have no choice.

Yesterday, I was talking to a German woman who had fled from Berlin just before the Russians. Why do you think she did it? This is what she told me. "I knew the Americans would be much better." This woman is about 35, perhaps more. Please don't be angry with me for talking to her. The only reason I talk to these people is to find out what they are thinking. Each and every one will try to give you a sad story.

This woman did. Here is what else she said about the bombings, and I quote. "I believe it was nothing but ruthless murdering of civilians." I then asked her who started it all, and she was silent for a few seconds. "We did [the Germans]," she said. I asked her about the bombing of London and strafing of civilians in England, France, and other countries, but she had no answer.

By this time, she was not talking, so I brought up politics. This always causes them to talk and get hot under the collar, and she was no exception. When I asked her about the Nazi government, she said, "It was good at first because it provided work for everyone." I told her that was true, but what kind of work? I asked, and without waiting for an answer, I told her, "Sure, they were building armament plants and super highways. Were the people blind as to what this would lead them into?" She had no answer.

When I asked about Hitler, she said, "Hitler is not German, he is Austrian." She does not believe he is dead. I asked her if she was going to stay in Austria. She answered, "I am German. I am going back to Germany." What in the hell can you say to people like that?

They're playing "Stay as Sweet as You Are" on the radio. Do you like it? Must close for now. Write often.

Always yours,
David

Mittersill, Austria
July 21, 1945

My Dearest,

I've had a very good day, and this evening has been swell considering I've had to do without you.

After supper, I went for a bike ride for a few miles out into the country. If I could only give you the picture of how beautiful it was, but then, I can't. When I returned from the bike ride, I went for a little walk down by the river. It was so quiet down there, and as I walked across the small footbridge, I came upon an artist drawing the small bridge and its surroundings. I watched for about 20 minutes, and for my money, he was pretty good.

The best of all is the fact that when I returned from my walk, I had a letter from you. So tonight, my morale is soaring in the blue. *Happy* isn't even the word for it. As you might say, I'm out of this world. They just read "My Sweetheart" over the radio. Do you like it, Lou? I do. I seldom miss this broadcast.

So you read the 101st will be over here for another year? Ha. What they probably meant was that we would be here throughout this year. God, not another year, please! I think I shall be leaving Austria very soon. I repeat, I think.

Enclosed are a few pages of a book *Dachau*.[35] No doubt you've heard of it. I'll keep sending it a few pages at a time until I send it

---

[35] The army published the gruesome photos taken of the genocide aftermath of the Dachau Concentration Camp. The book cover and introduction can be found in the "Battles, Campaigns, and Photograph" section. Dad kept the book. As he said, "One day, people will say it never happened, and I have the proof that it did."

all. Some of it isn't very nice. But I wish every person in the world could be given a copy of it to read. There are no doubts in my mind at all about it not being true.

Write often, sweetheart, and good night.

Always yours,
David

This book was dedicated to the Holocaust Memorial Museum in Maitland, Florida, by our mother after Dad passed away in January 1999.

The book "Comes A Soldier's Whisper" and some of the original letters have been donated and are on display at the Holocaust Memorial Museum in Maitland, Florida & The Military Museum of Kissimmee in Kissimmee, Florida for the preservation of history.

Auxerre, France
August 9, 1945

My Darling,

Today is a big day for the people of the world with Russia's entry into the war with Japan or, should I say, against Japan.

I believe it will mean the end of the war in the near future, and this new bomb. Well, you know of it, and I don't want to talk about it.

I really have a treat in front of me, a real American Coca Cola and a Clark candy bar. It's hard to believe. It's been so long. Darling, I believe it's best you don't send me any Christmas packages. Perhaps I'm taking a long chance, but I think this guy's going to be home for Christmas. I wonder what it will be like. I hardly think we will be the shy kids we were two years ago.

Yes, darling, you have had many chances to change your mind about me. I'm very happy that you still feel the same. May you never change your mind. For two years, we have been together. You've always been in my dreams and prayers. Yes, I've prayed. Many times, I lie in a muddy hole and have taken your picture out of my wallet. You have been through all kinds of hell with me. It sort of seemed that it helped while sweating out the next blast of shells.

So you decided to sort through all of the letters I've written to you? Well, you'll have to read some of them to me when I come home. I'll be surprised, no doubt, as to some of the things I've written. But I wouldn't take any of it back, good or bad. I hardly believe there is much bad in them though.

Darling, I'm so glad you feel the way you do about the racial problems of today. At least we shouldn't be fighting over that.

I want my children to be brought up to feel that they are equal and not to hate people because they are black. Oh, I can't really explain it here on paper. But I'm sure you know what I mean. As you said, we wouldn't have a large racial problem as we have today if the parents didn't teach their children about it.

Enclosed is one regimental insignia. Please take care of it as I have been trying for a long time to get one. You may think it's gruesome-looking, but we're proud of it: bat wings, skull, and parachute.

Always yours,
David

Auxerre, France
August 16, 1945

My Darling,

Well, we had another parade today. I hate the routine ones. This was for the third anniversary of the division. We have lost General Taylor. He's been given a job at West Point.

The five o'clock news was very good. They said they would lower the points to 75. Who knows? I might be home soon. I won't believe it until I'm on US soil.

Lou, I think it best to let you have the kind of wedding you like. As you say, it's only once in a life time. I will say this, though, since you asked me. I don't desire a large formal affair. So with that in mind, I'll leave it to you. I'll be scared anyway. So it doesn't matter.

I haven't told you yet. But after finishing high school, I may go to a radio school in Chicago. I am very much interested in radio. For two years, that's been my job. I've learned quite a bit from it. Still there is much more to learn. I like it very much, and it will be a good business after the war. I may as well put my experience to use.

I wish we had our own home. There was a time when my family did have nice furniture and everything. That was when my mother was living. Then we lost our home through a fire. Dad lost his job in the oil fields, and after that, it just seemed like we started down hill and could never get on our feet again. It just broke my father's heart. Well, enough of my families troubles though.

According to the paper this morning, we, the 101st Airborne, will go to Berlin as army of occupation. Darling, I think I shall go crazy if I have to go back into Germany with those damn boneheads. I wouldn't mind if I was needed and they were ruling the Nazis with an iron fist. But they're not. They're treating them just like babies. I get so darn mad, I can't see straight.

It's going to be a great disappointment to many of our men if we have to go back to Germany because we've been promised we were coming home.

All my love,
David

Auxerre, France
August 25, 1945

My Dearest,

I'm a very lonesome guy tonight. Do you think you could cheer me up?

I received a letter from the principal of the high school back home. He gave me the number of credits and subjects needed to graduate. So I guess I'll get on the ball and finish it out to the end. I realize more and more every day that I must go back to school.

There is a beautiful moon out tonight, my dear. It's a full moon too and the kind of clouds around that really set it off. I wonder if you too are looking at it. We're so far apart and yet so close together.

I'm eating donuts and drinking coffee, hon. So if I mess up the paper a little, you'll know what it is. Johnny, that's one of my buddies, just played a record for us that he received from his girl. On one side, it was nice. She sang for him, and on the other side, she told him how much she loved him. I guess that's the best part of it for him was to hear her voice again.

I wish to tell you that the rumor now is that I sail next month. Some of the fellows say it came over the radio today. I did not hear it, however, so keep your fingers crossed.

Always yours,
David

Auxerre, France
August 26, 1945

My Darling,

I was in Paris for the weekend. I enjoyed myself very much. I went Saturday afternoon and came back Sunday night.

While in Paris, I went to see the family that gave me the red, white, and blue carnations for my birthday. Remember, they have a little girl named Michele who stayed with her grandparents? I found out much more about her parents. Before, I was pretty much in the dark. Her father has just returned home from being a German prisoner for two years. Her mother works for the government in Paris. They're very nice people.

On Saturday night, we went to an American movie, and Sunday, we just toured around the city starting at the Eiffel Tower (their home is very near).

I'm supposed to ship out this week. Of course, that doesn't mean I'm coming straight home. But it will mean that I'm on my way. So say a little prayer and keep your fingers crossed my dear. Perhaps your guy will soon be at home.

What I'm going to say may sound funny, and if you must laugh, don't let me know. As I sit here, I've been gazing at the moon, and honest, it seems like the old man is really up there with a kind old face and look of wisdom looking down on a peaceful world tonight instead of what he's been used to seeing. In a way, he looks as though he's smiling a little.

Well, my cherie, tomorrow's another day. Good night and sweet dreams.

Always yours,
David

PS: About coming home. That was a rumor and is cold as ice. So we all got excited over nothing.

Auxerre, France
August 27, 1945

My Dearest,

I have my record player going. I'll bet I've played these darn records a million times. But I still like to hear some of them.

That is something we must have, darling, and a good collection too. These things sound like a dream, a home of our own and children; so far, it remains just that.

It will make me very happy, darling, if you will send little Michele something, and clothes might be good. I'll tell you why. Her grandmother bought enough material for a dress, and it cost 750 francs. Darling, that is $15 in American money. It's hard to believe, isn't it?

No, there's no sense in having your picture taken now or anything else for Christmas because I think I shall be at home by then or very soon after. God but that is a long time.

Lou, I want to marry you soon after I return, more than I can tell you. But I want you to really think it over because I must finish school, which means we will be pretty tied down if married.

I have received the number of credits I must have and the subjects I must take. I've applied for this army course, and they only have one subject on the list that I can take. This army education is just a bunch of propaganda for the people at home. The only person who is getting anything out of it is the guy who already has a couple of years of college.

Must close for now. Please write often.

Always yours,
David

Auxerre, France
August 29, 1945

My Dearest,

I'll be so glad when I can be near you and we won't have to depend upon a letter to reach us.

We are playing "Flying Home" on the record player. I sure wish that were true. It's by Harry James, and I really like it.

My job is a gold-bricking job now, darling. I'm operating a PA (public address system) a couple hours a day for the troop. It's so simple, well, perhaps for someone with skill. It's a good deal for me. So I won't complain.

Good night, my dear. Write often, please.

Always yours,
David

Auxerre, France
August 30 1945

My Dearest Lou,

I was over to see little Michele tonight. I just couldn't keep her quiet at all.

She's a regular little chatterbox. It's amazing how she learns, darling. Why, she can say many little things in English, and she gets a kick out of it too.

I'll bet you would laugh at us if you could peek through the window and see us trying out the French and English. But I do enjoy myself so much over there.

I wish she were ours, Lou. I know you would love her also.

Toujours Le Votre,
David

PS: I always get this French turned around every time. It's all backward to me.

Auxerre, France
September 2, 1945

My Dearest,

This is Sunday night. This afternoon I spent down by the river at
the beer parades, swimming a while and drinking some beer.

It's quite nice down there. From my table, I could leap right into
the water. Just yell "Garcon," and you have a waiter. They play
many American songs and a few French ones too. I just want to
come home sweetheart.

"Ridin for a Fall" is the record playing now. Coming up will be
"Blue Champagne" with Glenn Miller, good dance music. I think
I will be coming home soon. I have 88 points now. So as soon as
they start shipping again or, I should say, start on the ones who
have the points now. I should be among the first because I have
well over 80. I'm still sweating out getting another decoration.
But I don't ever expect to get it.

I'm so damn lonely, and it seems you should walk right out of your
picture. Perhaps we'll be together soon. How will we manage to
be married with my going to school and making a living? I think
we can make out. Together, we can do anything. But suppose a
little one comes along? Well, we can take care of it also. I know
we'll really be happy with a child and proud. Oh boy, did you ever
reconsider not having five children. That is a couple too many
isn't it?

Do you realize I've been a parachutist for two years this month?
I've been around different countries, and I've kicked and
knocked around. But I'm still together and ticking regular. My

heart misses a beat now and then when I think of you. And why shouldn't it?

Write often, Lou, please.

All my love and kisses,
David

Auxerre, France
September 7, 1945

My Dearest,

No letter from you for a couple of days. I guess you think I expect too much. I know how you must feel when you don't hear from me.

I suppose you have heard the news about the points. I was processed again today with all my points now. I have 88 according to today's paper. I should be home by Christmas, darling. Keep your fingers crossed for me. God, it would be wonderful to be at home for Christmas. I want very much to be at home with the kids, and yet, I also want to be home with you. Guess we'll have to work that one out together.

Next week we have a tactical jump. I guess the brass figure they must get their extra $50 from us. As far as I'm concerned, they can keep it. As long as the war was going on, I was willing to do all these things. In fact, I volunteered for many things because I wanted to be there, and I figured I was doing my part. But now that the war is over, why must they take men who will soon be civilians and endanger their lives and limbs? I just can't see it.

Write often, darling. Be seeing you soon, I hope.

Always yours,
David

Auxerre, France
September 11, 1945

My Darling,

You asked just how soon I'd be home, darling. I don't know and doubt if anyone else does.

Some of the boys think we'll leave the outfit around the last of the month or the first of October. I don't know what to say. They've put in for a school that's in Warton, England. If it comes through before my chance to come home does, then I'll go to England for about ten weeks.

Please don't be angry with me. It means a lot to me. And after almost two years, a couple of months shouldn't make any difference now. However, I'm not sure I'll get to go. They haven't promised me anything yet.

Darling, I must close for now. Please write often. Give my regards to the family.

Love and kisses,
David

Auxerre, France
September 13, 1945

My Darling,

I received your wonderful letter of September 8th, and that's pretty good time. I hope my letters are getting to you just as good.

Well, I've been a pretty busy lad today, hon, or I should say, this afternoon. I went for a plane ride and watched the fellows' jump and, later, rode out to the drop zone and took some pictures. I hope they come out because I had some beautiful shots. I wish you could see an actual jump. It's really something to watch as the men come piling out of the planes.

Darling, I like your idea of a small church wedding. That's really okay with me. I drink once in a while. But I don't want any drinking at my wedding or after it. I seldom drink anyway unless I'm in a crowd that does. So don't worry about me, darling. I don't have the habit. The only bad habit I have is smoking, and I've cut myself down until I get along easy on seven packs a week.

Well, things still point to my getting out of here soon. I don't know when, and no one else is sure. The army program is good for the morale of the people back home, but it's no darn good for the soldier. I hope the schooling or the GI Bill of Rights isn't like this, or I won't even mess with it. I hope I can take advantage of it though because after we're married, there are many other uses to which I can use the money I've saved.

About you working after we're married, I'm not going to be old-fashioned about it. If you want to work while I'm going to school, then I say go ahead. You're quite right when you say we don't know what's ahead of us—not another Depression, I hope. I can just remember the last one. As long as you're job is easy, then there's no reason why you shouldn't continue to work if you want to. If I can take advantage of the GI Bill of Rights and go to school, we can make out okay with the two of us pulling together. We'll do okay. I'm not worried about that at all.

Stop. (News flash.) A hot rumor just came in. Men with over 85 points as of VJ day leave between October 21st and 25th. You know, one of these rumors will be true one of these days, I hope. Oh, I want to come home to you so very much. I hope you don't think I've changed very much. It seems I have a terrible temper anymore, much worse than I used to have. But anyone would have if they stayed around here.

So we have an invitation to visit one of your bosses some evening, we'll see. I'm sorry to hear about his son.

So you think I've developed? I'm still a big rawboned lug with long arms and wavy blond hair. I don't have to have a good build. I'm just big enough that I scare people to death. Ha.

Do you realize that in a few days, the 17th to be exact, I was on a plane riding to Holland? God, it's all a dream in a way. One year ago, for a few seconds that day, I thought I would never see you again, darling. But here I am, sweating out a trip home. It's wonderful to be alive.

Must close for now, my love.

Always yours,
David

Le Havre, France
October 1, 1945

My Darling,

I'm now in Le Havre, France, after my leave in England. Once again, I'm very lonesome for you.

It's beautiful at this camp, Lou. We're way out in the country, and the camp is sort of back in the woods. You can really tell it's the fall of the year. The leaves are turning all the beautiful colors that one finds this time of the year.

I'm out in the grass writing this. I wish you were with me. I have my portable with me, and the music is something wonderful.

I heard a rumor last night that some of the high-point men have shipped out. If they have, I'll pull my hair out—at least, I'll feel like it. If it's true, I shouldn't be around very long after I return to my unit.

I didn't write to you while I was in England, darling. I spent all but two days traveling, and those I spent in London. I didn't like London very well. I saw everything possible in those two days, including the movie *GI Joe*. I liked it very much but felt like leaving a couple of times. Among the other places I visited were St. Paul's Cathedral, Buckingham Palace, Tower of London Bridge, Rainbow Corner, and Westminster Abby. A place known as Petticoat Lane is quite famous in London. It's only open on Sunday morning. It is said that before the war, one could buy anything from a pen to a suit. After seeing it, I can well believe it.

Well, darling, I must close as I leave here for Paris in about an hour and stay in Paris until tomorrow afternoon and on to Auxerre.

Always yours,
David

Auxerre, France
October 8, 1945

Dearest Lou,

Well, I'm back in this dear little French town and not a bit happy about it either. Sure glad I have little Michele to go and see. She's too little to understand my worries. But it's good to be with her and do things for her.

I'm in a bad temper tonight. So if I say something I shouldn't, please don't hold it against me. I got several letters from you today, six to be exact. I'm always more than grateful for a few words from you.

You said in one of your letters that if I were to return now, it would be next to impossible for you to get a leave from your job. My dear, if your silly old job is that much more important than I am after our being apart for two years, I hope you only realize what that did to me as I read it. If you can't get off when I return, then just remember it's your own decision. I can always spend my leave down home with my grandmother and the kids. And that's what I'll do if you can't get off.

After two years of miserable hell in this godforsaken country, living and thinking and dreaming, praying for the day when I could hold you in my arms, kiss you and hold you close, telling you I love you and how much you mean to me, and now you write such things as "I don't want to get married for a year or so. I'm sure to lose my job if I do. I'm sure I couldn't get off if you were to come home now." Well, I'm afraid coming home now doesn't mean what it did to me a few months ago. Perhaps you don't understand my saying that. I doubt if you do.

I believe we're both pretty miserable, my darling, waiting so long and everything. It just seems like everyone is coming home except me. If I could, I would come home tonight. But I'm afraid it isn't up to me.

Must close for now. Give my regards to Mom and Dad and the kids.

Always yours,
David

CHAPTER XIII

Marching Home Again

Days are never the same as before
Since he has gone away to war
Since he has taken the burden too
To help his country see it through

He's one of thousands in the ranks
To man the ships, the guns, the tanks
He has his jokes; he has his fun
But he's always aware that there is work to be done

We're looking forward to the day
When he'll be coming home to stay
When countries are free from tyrannies reign
They'll come marching home again

And what a triumph that stride will be
When they return to the Land of the Free

—Betty Lou

Auxerre, France
October 16, 1945

My Darling,

I'm very happy and excited tonight. I leave for Belgium in the morning. Of course, I realize that it is only the first part of my journey home. But it's a start, darling, a move closer to you.

It may take weeks—that we don't know. I'm going straight to Antwerp, so I'm hoping for the best. It's a big port, and who knows? I will probably have to seat it out at least a couple of weeks in some camp nearby and a week or ten days for the trip home. Really, I expect about a month before I hit US soil. I'll keep writing until I leave.

I had hoped for a letter from you yesterday or today, but no luck. So I hope my journey is a fast one. You know, I wonder just how much my girl has changed—not much, I hope. It's just so hard to realize I'm coming home after all of this.

Terry is leaving with me—or rather, he's in my group. His spirits are pretty high also. I figure we'll be in the US around November 10th. So keep your fingers crossed, darling.

Well, I haven't much to write tonight, Lou. It's late, and I want to get some sleep. We must get up at 4 in the morning.

So good night, hon.

Always yours.

Love and kisses,
David

Namur, Belgium
October 19, 1945

My Darling,

It's been a long time now, hon, and it's really hard to believe that I've started on my way home. After all this time, it just doesn't seem true.

From here I will go to Antwerp for the boat ride home. I'll probably stay here about ten days and at the port about seven to ten days. The trip will be anything from five to twelve days, depending upon the ship we get.

Terry is here with me. It's really good to be going home with him. He's such a good guy; it's pleasant to be with him. Life is pretty good here so far. I'm on KP duty tomorrow. Honest, I can't remember when the last time was that I had kitchen duty. You won't make me do that after we're married, will you?

Still have my radio with me. It's really worthwhile. I guess I'll bring it home if I can get it there. I wonder what the future holds for me, Lou. Will we be married very soon? It seems that you'd rather not be. Of course, that's up to you. I'm ready to settle down myself. Somehow, I'm a little afraid of myself coming back to you now, Betty Lou. I'm very much in love with you. Of course, I want to go to school. I want to be able to give you a good home and everything that goes with it. If we're married very soon after my return, we couldn't have all the things we want. I'm not saying we wouldn't be happy. I know we would be in spite of how things turn out.

I still think we could get married and I could finish school. If you want to go ahead and work, then you could. I'm sure that within eight months to a year, I will be on my feet. We'll really be able to talk this over when I get home.

Must close for tonight, darling, so I can get a good night's sleep. Don't write anymore, Lou. You'll just have to wait until I get home.

Love and kisses,
David

Antwerp, Belgium
October 28, 1945

My Darling,

Well, I'm now at the port. They say we'll be here anywhere from three to ten days. It's pretty good here, no details yet though.

The warships and air carriers they brought over here should be a great help in keeping the troops moving. I think I'll be with you for Thanksgiving, hon.

This is Sunday morning, and they've been playing such songs as "My Indiana Home" and "White Christmas" over the loudspeaker system. They're making us all homesick, not that we're not anyway. Still it's good to hear those good old songs.

It's beautiful here on the coast today. The sun is out very bright, and a blue sky and a sharp wind coming in from the sea makes one feel like living. And now that I'm coming home, I really feel like it, and after two years, it's no wonder.

The group I'm with is all Hoosier boys. They're from all over the state, only two from my outfit. We're all from the same division though. It's hard to realize we're really coming home after all this time, coming back for good. I wonder just how many of us will really want to settle down.

I'd advise you to do some serious thinking before I return, darling. Remember that I love you, and at present, I feel the same as I always have. I say "at present" because anything can happen once we're together again. I'm sure everything will be okay though.

The more I think about our marriage as I return closer to home, the more I agree with you about not being married right away. Why, you might not like me in civilian clothes even. There are many things you don't know about me, Lou, and vice versa. You said some time ago that you couldn't keep your job if you were married. I couldn't very well work and go to school if we're married either. Oh, there are many things, darling. We'll just have to talk them over when I'm home.

Must close for now, darling. If I'm here for a few days, I'll write again. If not, you'll know I'm on my way home.

Love and kisses,
David

Petersburg, Indiana
December 1, 1945

My Darling,

First of all, I'm pretty darn lonesome down here.[36]

But I've been pretty busy, and I don't mean maybe getting things fixed up for my grandmother, brothers, and sisters. I haven't even visited my relatives yet and don't think I will either. They know where I live.

Darling, I guess I'll be down here for another week. I've got plenty to do. I don't know what you'll think of me. But I've bought a home here in my hometown of Petersburg, not that I'd ever live here, but it's for Grandma and the kids.

Grandmother didn't want me to do it after I told her about us getting married sometime in the future. But I went ahead anyway. I can never repay her for taking care of my brothers and sisters since my dad died in 1943. When you come down here with me for Christmas, you will see some changes.

I'm going to Washington tomorrow and see your grandparents and also going to do some shopping over there. I wish you were along, darling. You could be a great help to me.

Sunday I'm going to wash all the woodwork inside and do some painting, etc. There won't be any wallpapering until the spring though it's in pretty good shape. Oh, there are a million things I could write to you about it.

---

[36] Dad decided to return to his hometown first to take care of his grandmother, who had been caring for his four younger siblings after his dad died in 1943.

Hon, your letter was so nice, I felt like crying. I just wanted to come back right away. It seems like we're already married. God knows I miss you enough.

Everyone's well and quite happy. I've talked my brother, Johnny, into going on to school, so even I feel pretty good.

I have to get up early in the morning to catch the bus for Washington. Good night, Lou. Give my love to Mother and Dad and the kids.

Forever yours,
David

Petersburg, Indiana
December 4, 1945

My Darling,

Guess you must feel that I've forgotten you, far from that.

Believe it or not, I've been working. I've got everything moved now. There's really a big difference over here, both inside and out. It isn't the best, but I can say it's clean. That's the important thing.

It's now a little after eleven. My sister, Irene, just came home from work. Everyone else is in bed.

I wish I were with you, darling. It's okay here during the day because I'm busy, but late at night I'm lonesome, which is putting it mild. I'm coming back up this Saturday or Monday. Then we'll come back down here for Christmas. I do hope everything works out okay. It'll be so nice to have you here with me and my brothers and sisters.

I must close for tonight. I was over to see your grandparents. They're swell. I stayed about an hour.

All my love,
David

Petersburg, Indiana
December 6, 1945

My Darling,

I got a very sweet letter from you today. I can't tell you how happy I am that you feel as I do and agree with what I've done. It means a lot to me, hon.

As you said, our lives are just beginning, and we'll never miss what I've put out here. The kids are all growing up now, and it's more of an investment than anything else.

I just can't think or have any idea at all as what you've gotten me for Christmas, and guess I'll just have to wait. I also found something for you today. I'm sure you'll like it. It'll take a few days to get it. But I assure you it's worth waiting for.

Hon, I hope you're not angry at me for this. But I've decided not to come back up as I had planned. There's quite a bit to be done around here, and after Christmas, I won't be back until around spring. And if I don't do it, it just won't be done. It's hard for me to stay here, though, when I know I could be with you. I think you understand.

Do you want me to come up around the 20th so I can come down with you, darling? I can't see you making the trip yourself. I think it's best if I come up. It doesn't cost much, and I can travel with you.

I must close for now, cherie. Good night, my darling.

Forever yours,
David

Petersburg, Indiana
December 10, 1945

My Darling,

Just a few lines tonight. It's so lonesome here. My sister Betty's been singing her Christmas carols for me. She doesn't know them too good yet though.

Everything is coming along pretty good. It's cold though and snowed a little today. I'm feeling good now. So far the kids haven't missed any school.

Grandmother is going through the cards and letters that you have written her. I think she's showed every one of them to me. Thanks, hon. She really thinks you and the family are about it. I went to Washington one night with some of my old pals. They really gave me the devil. They thought I was stepping out on you. I didn't get in until about two o'clock.

Lou, this little sister of mine is really a tomboy. She plays tackle football with the boys, and she's just as rough as the next one. I asked her what she wanted for Christmas, and right away, she said, "A football and two pairs of overall pants." Now how's that for a ten-year-old girl? I almost fell over!

I'd sure love to be up there with you, darling. After Christmas, we'll be together regular. I'll sure be happy then.

Must close for now, hon. But I'll be up to see you about the 20th or 21st.

Forever yours,
David

THE SOLDIER'S GRAVE

Breathe not a *whisper* here;
The place where thou dost stand is hallowed ground;
In silence gather near this upheaved mound -
Around the soldier's bier.

Here Liberty may weep,
And Freedom pause in her unchecked career,
To pay the sacred tribute of a tear
O'er the pale warrior's sleep.

That arm now cold in death,
But late on glory's field triumphant bore
Our country's flag; that marble brow once bore
The victor's fadeless wreath.

Rest soldier, sweetly rest;
Affection's gentle hand shall deck thy tomb
With flowers and chaplets of unfading bloom
Be laid upon thy breast.

-Author unknown

Just A Country Boy

Epilogue

It is important to note here that many soldiers displayed signs of PTSD (post-traumatic stress disorder) after WWII, which was depicted in the American movie *The Best Years of Our Lives*, made in 1946, about three veterans experiencing difficulties returning to civilian life, much in the same way our soldiers of today experience.

Although the United States government has many wonderful rehabilitation programs now in place for the American veterans of war, we need a *boot camp kind of push* to consistently improve the transition of all soldiers as well as the families of those soldiers' ultimate transition back to civilian life, working through each phase of emotions—or lack thereof—somewhat the way a diver decompresses slowly before resurfacing.

My father believed wholeheartedly that the United States must maintain our military force to protect our life, liberty, freedom, and justice for all. Dad would say throughout his lifetime, "Another world war could happen again and on American soil. We cannot let our guard down."

In order to protect our nation and our freedoms, we must have a strong military, a strong base, and a strong people. We owe this to our forefathers, descendants, ourselves, and to all of those who follow in our footsteps. This in no way need interfere with our continual efforts to question, understand, and learn to coexist with other nations. There will always be a national financial debt and deficit to contend with. But should we intentionally and/or knowingly allow our military to be reduced, preventing them from protecting this country and our allies, it could be a very long road to perdition and a ledger that may only be balanced with our demise.

Freedom can come at a great price, often with the lives of our loved ones. But for those who sacrifice their lives or health in the fight for our country, we can reciprocate by offering donations and our time. There are many veteran programs to take care of our returning soldiers, but they funding and volunteers to persevere.

Dad was honorably discharged in November 1945 and married his sweetheart, our mother, in March 1946 and went on to have five children and eleven grandchildren. They made a life together in Portage, Indiana. Dad worked in the Gary steel mills, enduring several strikes. He then worked at various auto body shops until opening his own auto body shop called Portage Auto Craft.

Dad went on to serve as President of the Izzac Walton League between 1962-1963 for the preservation of land and water, something near and dear to his heart. While in office as the Portage Chamber of Commerce President, he addressed the association by saying, "I was happy to shake the sand of the Normandy beaches out of my boots 20 years ago, and I'll be happier still to shake the sand of a barren stretch of land out of my shoes to give Indiana her gateway to the world."

In 1964, Dad began working for National Can Corporation in Chicago, Illinois as the Manager of Safety and Industrial Hygiene. He presented speeches, implemented new safety procedures and traveled extensively to the vast company distribution plants to ensure that those procedures were adhered to. He retired in

1987. For many years, Dad would enjoy fishing, boating and his motorcycle trips.

I am proud to say that my father grew and became whom he could be-a loving, understanding, articulate, and soft-spoken man who served in public office, utilizing his communication skills, and writing safety procedures for the protection of his employees.

My father evolved from that once frightened and angry young man during and after the war to someone that sought to methodically question, understand, and communicate differences toward a common goal.

With that said, I will leave the reader with my father's quote from his retirement speech.

As we prepare for tomorrow's challenge, let us listen and learn, let us explore and question and understand.
                                        —David Clinton Tharp

Footnotes

1. During the Great Depression, CCC stood for Civilian Conservation Corps. This government program was the part of President Franklin Roosevelt's New Deal effort that dealt with alleviating severe unemployment in the United States. The program ran from 1933 to 1942. Dad entered the service through Fort Benjamin in Harrison, Indiana. After completing basic training, he transferred to technical training in Colorado.

2. See envelope photo in "Campaign, Battles, and Photographs" section.

3. War bonds are government-issued savings bonds, which are used to finance a war or a military action. In the United States, the last official war bond was the Series E bond issued during the Second World War. War bonds generate capital for the federal government, and they make civilians feel involved in their national militaries. Exhortations to buy war bonds are often accompanied with appeals to patriotism and conscience.

4. Army paratrooper training location airborne school is held at Fort Benning in Columbus, Georgia. Airborne trainees are housed in the airborne barracks during training. The location of the training

is on the main post at Fort Benning and can be easily identified by the 250-foot-tall airborne towers. Airborne training is three weeks long, though some soldiers may be on holdover for several weeks, waiting for a training slot in the school. Somewhere along the line, Dad was changed over from the Air Force to Army Paratroopers most likely as replacement to fallen soldiers overseas.

5. During the D-day invasion of World War II, many soldiers were sent with a pigeon beneath their coats. This was a period of radio silence, so the use of pigeons for relaying messages was optimal. The pigeons were able to send back information on German gun positions on the Normandy beaches. Thirty-two pigeons were awarded the prestigious Dickin Medal, Britain's highest award for animal valor. Recipients included a bird named G. I. Joe, who flew twenty miles in twenty minutes with a message that stopped US planes from bombing an Italian town that was occupied by British forces. Army Pigeons in World War I and II | Suite101.

6. A group of women and men dedicated to preserving the history of the United Service Organizations (USO) during the World War Two time period. WW2 USO—Stateside Operations—Living History.

7. The moral of a soldier is critical to keeping his spirit intact.

8. Here it is, in a soldier's own words: the best thing that family can do to keep his moral up is to write letters.

9. My great-grandmother Amelia, my father's grandmother, took in all his five siblings after his father died in 1943 from a heart attack. His father made him promise to keep all the kids together and avoid adoption should anything happen to him.

10. D-Day—Operation Neptune.
The 101st Airborne Division first saw combat during the Normandy invasion, 6 June 1944. The division, as part of the VII Corps assault,

jumped in the dark morning before H-Hour to seize positions west of Utah Beach. Given the mission of anchoring the corps' southern flank, the division was also to eliminate the German's secondary beach defenses, allowing the seaborne forces of the 4th Infantry Division, once ashore, to continue inland. The SCREAMING EAGLES were to capture the causeway bridges that ran behind the beach between St. Martin-de-Varreville and Pouppeville. In the division's southern sector, it was to seize the la Barquette lock and destroy a highway bridge northwest of the town of Carentan and a railroad bridge farther west. At the same time, elements of the division were to establish two bridgeheads on the Douve River at le Port, northeast of Carentan. The 101st Airborne Division During WW II—Overview.

11. The hardest part of parachuting was landing on the ground. Landing can be difficult depending on the speed and height of the plane. On D-day, a lot of paratroopers received injuries because the C-47s were flying at 150 mph and were a lot closer to the ground than they should have been.

12. Jerry was a nickname for Germans during the war.

13. June 6, 1944, the day the Allied powers crossed the English Channel and landed on the beaches of Normandy, France, beginning the liberation of Western Europe from Nazi control during World War II. Within three months, the northern part of France would be freed and the invasion force would be preparing to enter Germany, where they would meet up with Soviet forces moving in from the east. D-day—History.com, This Day in History—6/6/1944.

14. Dad caught a bullet in his leg and had surgery for his kneecap many years later.

15. Dad was praying that he never receive a Cluster as that would mean another injury. Dad, in fact, went on to receive that Cluster for his Purple Heart in the Battle of the Bulge. In US Military,

Oak Leaf Clusters on ANY medal indicate multiple awards of that medal.

16. *Yank*, the army weekly, was one of the finest military publications of World War II. Yank, The Army Weekly: World War Two Magazine | Writinghood.

17. Operation Market-Garden was conducted September 17-25, 1944, in an attempt to capture bridges over the Rhine. Operation Market-Garden—Operation Market Garden 1944.

18. In WW2, newspapers and television news were censored. Censorship is when the government decides what or what not to show the people. Government considered it necessary in order to boost morale, but it was also a dangerous precedent because it violated 1st Amendment free speech. The trend of censorship has been a common theme in wars throughout America and across the world and is a dangerous side effect for war.

19. Christmas Day 1944 was a horrendous day for the 502, 401 & 463 filled with see saw battle overcoming serious odds to keep the Germans from getting into Bastogne. This was one of the hardest fought battles of the siege. Dad was always sad around Christmas. We thought it was because his mother passed away around the holidays. But upon reading his letters, we discovered that Christmas in particular was a somber time for him for many reasons. But this did not deter him from giving us a fresh-cut pine tree every year.

Leo Barron and Don Cygan give a compelling and detailed account of the Five-O-Deuce's gallant and unrelenting defense of Champs and Rolle that Christmas in 1944 in the book, "NO SILENT NIGHT."

20. The V-mail system, named after the WWII "V for *victory*" symbol, was developed to help reduce the shipping space needed for the

massive increase in mail being sent between American armed forces overseas and their family and friends at home. Victory Mail of the Second World War | A Continuous Lean.

The letters dated January 2, 3, 4, 5, 7 & 22nd of 1945 were originally found with 1944 dates but corrected to avoid confusion in the timeline & proper sequence. Dad was recovering from a shell shock injury in The Battle of the Bulge in December 1944 & in his confusion continued to write 1944, when it was really 1945 . . .

21. Little Dave, or Davey, mentioned throughout is a reference to a son he hopes to have one day.

22. A bonus, something for nothing, as in "What do you want—egg in your beer?" This expression dates from about 1940 and became widespread during World War II. The origin is unknown since adding egg to beer does not improve the taste. What does "egg in your beer" mean? | "egg in your beer" meaning.

23. A 4F was a draft classification that meant medically unfit to serve. What did a 4H military rating mean in World War 2?—Yahoo.

24. *First Allied Airborne Army.* During its eight-month existence, the First Allied Airborne Army would execute two large-scale airborne assaults, Operation MARKET and Operation VARSITY. An important addition to the SHAEF forces came from the establishment of the First Allied Airborne Army in August 1944. The First Allied Airborne Army was formed as a major command operationally subordinate to SHAEF and not under an army group. The Airborne Army was established to coordinate the air and ground forces required for airborne operations. To assist in the conduct of airborne operations and to simplify command difficulties, the Airborne Army was an integrated US-British headquarters.

First Allied Airborne Army—GlobalSecurity.org—Reliable.

25. Dad was a Hoosier and country boy from southern Indiana.

26. Terry and Dad became lifetime friends. Terry, whose real name is Charles Eckman, visited our family often. He called Dad the Golden Warrior.

27. The Presidential Unit Citation is a senior unit award granted to military units that have performed an extremely meritorious or heroic act, usually in the face of an armed enemy. Presidential Unit Citation—Wikipedia, the free encyclopedia.

28. A Bronze Star Medal is for individual military decoration and the fourth highest award for bravery, heroism, or meritorious service. Bronze Star Medal (Model #124 ARBS)—USA Military Medals.

29. The so-called Eagle's Nest was built as a teahouse for Adolf Hitler's fiftieth birthday. Perched on a mountain summit, its unusual position makes of the daring project a unique engineering feat. History of Hitler's Eagle's Nest, the Kehlsteinhaus.

30. Dad served as a radio operator for Colonel Cole, Colonel Michaelis and Colonel Steve Chappius. His position as a radio communications man with Regimental Headquarters was very demanding especially when relaying critical orders and directives from high-ranking colonels.

31. Ack-ack: Anti-aircraft guns usually with multi-barrels with 4 or 6 barrels

32. Paratroopers went through some of the most vigorous and difficult training in the war and were considered among the elite soldiers in the war.

33. Displaced persons were mostly Eastern Europeans: people who were unable or unwilling to return to their native countries after WWII. Displaced Person Transportation, post-World War II.

34. There were signs of PTSD, post-traumatic stress disorder, during and after the war. Although there were some programs implemented, it is nothing as we know it today. Dad would suffer from terrible headaches over the years and would always moan in his sleep.

35. The army published the gruesome photos taken of the genocide aftermath of the Dachau Concentration Camp. The book cover and introduction can be found in the "Battles, Campaigns, and Photograph" section. Dad kept the book. As he said, "One day, people will say it never happened, and I have the proof that it did." This book was dedicated to the Holocaust Memorial Museum in Maitland, Florida, by our mother after Dad passed away in January 1999.

    The book "Comes A Soldier's Whisper" and some of the original letters have been donated and are on display at the Holocaust Memorial Museum in Maitland, Florida & The Military Museum of Kissimmee in Kissimmee, Florida for the preservation of history.

36. Dad decided to return to his hometown first to take care of his grandmother, who had been caring for his four younger siblings after his dad died in 1943.